CAMBRIDGE LIBRARY COLLECTION

Books of enduring scholarly value

Travel and Exploration

The history of travel writing dates back to the Bible, Caesar, the Vikings and the Crusaders, and its many themes include war, trade, science and recreation. Explorers from Columbus to Cook charted lands not previously visited by Western travellers, and were followed by merchants, missionaries, and colonists, who wrote accounts of their experiences. The development of steam power in the nineteenth century provided opportunities for increasing numbers of 'ordinary' people to travel further, more economically, and more safely, and resulted in great enthusiasm for travel writing among the reading public. Works included in this series range from first-hand descriptions of previously unrecorded places, to literary accounts of the strange habits of foreigners, to examples of the burgeoning numbers of guidebooks produced to satisfy the needs of a new kind of traveller - the tourist.

The Voyage of Sir Henry Middleton to Bantam and the Maluco Islands

The publications of the Hakluyt Society (founded in 1846) made available edited (and sometimes translated) early accounts of exploration. The first series, which ran from 1847 to 1899, consists of 100 books containing published or previously unpublished works by authors from Christopher Columbus to Sir Francis Drake, and covering voyages to the New World, to China and Japan, to Russia and to Africa and India. This volume (published in 1855) is devoted to an account of Sir Henry Middleton's voyage to the Molucca Islands in 1604–6 on behalf of the East India Company. The appendices contain transcriptions of various documents relating to the voyage, including James I's commission authorising the expedition, the king's letters to the various rulers Middleton was likely to encounter (including one where the address to 'the greate and mightie kinge of . . .' was left to be filled in should occasion arise), and letters from these rulers which Middleton conveyed back to London.

Cambridge University Press has long been a pioneer in the reissuing of out-of-print titles from its own backlist, producing digital reprints of books that are still sought after by scholars and students but could not be reprinted economically using traditional technology. The Cambridge Library Collection extends this activity to a wider range of books which are still of importance to researchers and professionals, either for the source material they contain, or as landmarks in the history of their academic discipline.

Drawing from the world-renowned collections in the Cambridge University Library, and guided by the advice of experts in each subject area, Cambridge University Press is using state-of-the-art scanning machines in its own Printing House to capture the content of each book selected for inclusion. The files are processed to give a consistently clear, crisp image, and the books finished to the high quality standard for which the Press is recognised around the world. The latest print-on-demand technology ensures that the books will remain available indefinitely, and that orders for single or multiple copies can quickly be supplied.

The Cambridge Library Collection will bring back to life books of enduring scholarly value (including out-of-copyright works originally issued by other publishers) across a wide range of disciplines in the humanities and social sciences and in science and technology.

The Voyage of Sir Henry Middleton to Bantam and the Maluco Islands

Being the Second Voyage Set Forth by the Governor and Company of Merchants of London Trading into the East-Indies

Edited by Bolton Corney

CAMBRIDGE UNIVERSITY PRESS

Cambridge, New York, Melbourne, Madrid, Cape Town, Singapore,
São Paolo, Delhi, Dubai, Tokyo, Mexico City

Published in the United States of America by Cambridge University Press, New York

www.cambridge.org
Information on this title: www.cambridge.org/9781108008143

This edition first published 1855
This digitally printed version 2010

ISBN 978-1-108-00814-3 Paperback

WORKS ISSUED BY

The Hakluyt Society.

VOYAGE TO BANTAM AND THE MALUCO ISLANDS, 1604-6.

M.DCCC.LV.

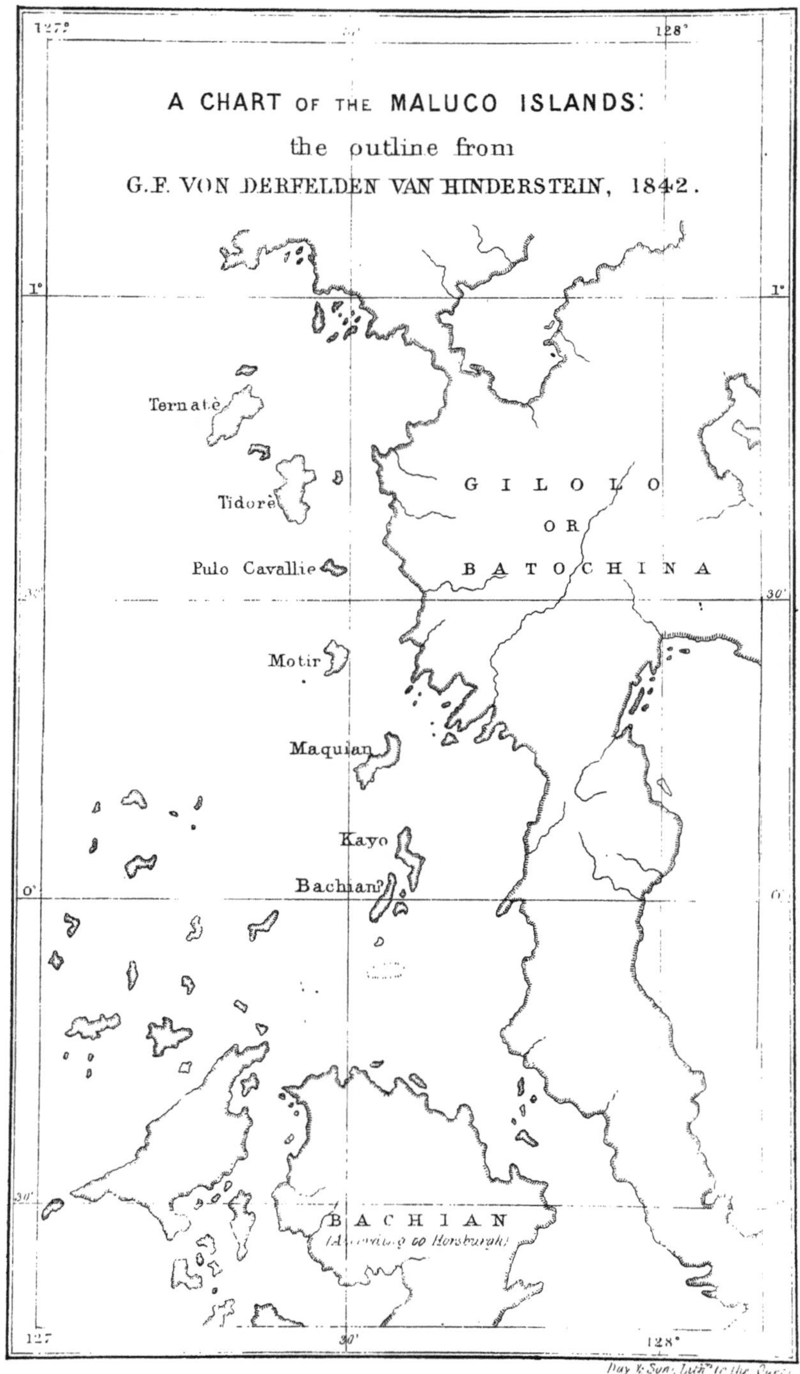

Day & Son, Lith.rs to the Queen

THE

VOYAGE

OF

SIR HENRY MIDDLETON

TO

BANTAM AND THE MALUCO ISLANDS;

BEING THE SECOND VOYAGE SET FORTH BY

THE GOVERNOR AND COMPANY OF MERCHANTS OF LONDON TRADING INTO THE EAST-INDIES.

FROM THE EDITION OF 1606.

Annotated and edited by

BOLTON CORNEY, M.R.S.L.

LONDON:

PRINTED FOR THE HAKLUYT SOCIETY.

M.DCCC.LV.

THE HAKLUYT SOCIETY.

CONTENTS.

CONTENTS.

ADVERTISEMENT.

Of the numerous examples of maritime enterprise which claim a notice in the history of the nation, none were more productive of exciting events, or of important results, than the early voyages which were set forth by the *Governor and company of merchants of London trading into the East-Indies*—who were incorporated by royal charter on the last day of the year 1600.

Nevertheless, in consequence of various adverse circumstances, the narratives of those voyages have remained in comparative obscurity ; and as no sufficient statement of the case has come before me, in despite of much earnest research, I shall report it in conformity with my own inquiries and impressions.

The venerable Hakluyt had completed his far-famed volumes, entitled *The principal navigations, voiages, traffiqves and discoueries of the English nation*, just before the associated merchants were favoured with their charter, and no augmented edition of the work was ever produced, nor any continuation of it on the same judicious and definite plan.

Now, the spirit of enterprise rather increased at the close of the sixteenth century. The voyages to Virginia and other parts of America, and into the north-western seas, were soon afterwards of frequent occurrence, and various *relations* of those voyages came out in the fugitive shape of pamphlets. The other hemisphere also attracted much attention ; and the energetic proceedings of the governor and committee of the East-India Company, acting in behalf of more than two hundred members, promised an ample and novel accession to the mass of nautical journals. The *Principal navigations*, in process of time, would therefore require a very considerable supplement.

It had been foreseen by Hakluyt that the *profession of divinitie*, and other *occasions*, might divert him from his geographical pursuits, and he was induced to nominate, as his editorial successor, master John Pory, late a student at Cambridge, who gave proof of his qualifications by a translation of Leo Africanus, which he undertook at the persuasion of Hakluyt, and dedicated to sir Robert Cecil, as the *first fruits* of his labours, in 1601. So far the prospect was cheering: I must now describe the adverse circumstances.

The *first fruits* of the labours of Pory proved to be the entire gathering ! A new scene of life presented itself, and its charms prevailed over his studious habits. He visited France, Italy, and Holland, and made two voyages to Virginia, where he held office as secretary to the colony, as a member of the council, and afterwards as a commissioner of inquiry.

He was also noted, as master George Sandys reports, for his "painful discoveries to the southward". He returned to England in 1624, and died before 1635.

I must now advert to the career of Hakluyt after the completion of his *Principal navigations* in 1600. The merit of those volumes must have been soon felt. He was appointed chaplain to sir Robert Cecil in 1601; received a prebend in the collegiate church of Westminster in 1602; and was made archdeacon of Westminster in 1603. With such preferments he could not have much spare time, but his geographical zeal was unabated. He edited two valuable works, and procured the publication of two others. Another service remains to be stated. He undertook the custody of the manuscript journals of the voyages and travels to which it was held unadvisable to give immediate publicity; comprising voyages to Virginia and to the north-western seas, and *all the East-India voyages from* 1601 *almost to the date of his decease in* 1616.

About the year 1620, under circumstances which are nowhere distinctly stated, the collections formed by Hakluyt came into the hands of the reverend Samuel Purchas, whose *Pilgrimage or relations of the world*, an unfinished work which was first published in 1613, had then reached its third edition. Now Purchas, instead of framing a continuation of the *Principal navigations*, as edited by Hakluyt, aspired to supersede those volumes by a new compilation, which should include the Hakluyt papers and his own collections. In consequence of this injudicious resolution he was compelled, as he admits, to *contract* and *epitomise* his vast materials. After much laborious application, made irksome by bodily infirmity, he published the results in 1625, in four folio volumes, with the quaint title of *Hakluytus posthumus, or Purchas his pilgrimes.*

It is in those rare and costly volumes, and under such unfavourable circumstances, that the early East-India voyages made their first and only appearance. The exceptions are, a brief *Discourse* of the voyage of sir James Lancaster in 1601, which is entirely omitted; and the *Voyage* of sir Henry Middleton in 1604, which is misplaced and mutilated. The *Report* of Robert Coverte is no exception to this statement: it is an account of land-travels and personal adventures.

Had due measures been adopted for the preservation of the unmutilated journals, no objection could have been made to *epitomisation.* I believe, however, they were left to the chance of destruction, and that most of them have perished! By whose authority were they successively entrusted to Hakluyt and Purchas? Why were they not claimed on the death of Purchas? It is my conviction that they were so entrusted by sir Thomas Smith, who was treasurer for Virginia, a patron of the north-western attempts, and governor of the East-India Company; and as to the second question, I must observe that sir Thomas Smith died on the 4th of September, 1625—in which year Purchas completed his *Pilgrimes*—and that Purchas himself died in the following year. Whatever be the feelings of individuals, they cannot transmit them to their heirs or official successors.

An estimate of the amount of mutilation committed by Purchas in the course of his editorial proceedings would be useless, if it were possible; but it seems incumbent on me to report how far the censure applies to the voyage in question. I believe the particulars will be read with surprise, if not with indignation. His treatment of Clayborne is stated in the notes, and shall not be repeated. With regard to the journal which forms the text of this volume, exclusive of the three royal letters, he compressed it into less than *one-twentieth part* of its real extent!

The sole unmutilated specimen of the early East-India voyages—with the slight exception before cited—and the sole record of the accomplishment of an object which was the principal stimulus to the formation of the East-India Company, must interest a wide circle of readers, and can only require to be made more accessible. The former edition is not in many hands—witness the declaration of the late Mr. Thomas Grenville: "It is so rare that I have not been able to trace any mention of it; nor have I ever seen another copy of it."

A narrative which occupies so limited a space, and is far from devoid of notes, cannot require many previous remarks, but some short memoranda may be desirable.

The fleet was composed of the Red Dragon, the Hector, the Ascension, and the Susan — *old ships* which had been repaired for the voyage. The Susan, which was lost on her return from Bantam, was a *rotten ship* when purchased. The burden of the four ships amounted to sixteen hundred tons. The number of men may be estimated at five hundred or more.

The principal officers, at the time of departure, were Henry Middleton, commander-in-chief, and captains David Middleton, Christopher Colthurst, Roger Stiles, and William Keeling. Henry Middleton, a native of Chester, went out with Lancaster in 1601. At Acheen he was appointed to the command of the Susan, and sent to Priaman, whence he carried home a cargo of pepper. His return was minuted the 21st of June 1603—which was near two months before the arrival of Lancaster. David Middleton, also a native of Chester, was his brother. Stiles died at Bantam. The Middletons, Colthurst, and Keeling, returned in safety.

The establishment of peace between England and Spain, the capture of the Portuguese fort at Amboina by the Dutch, and their success at Tidorè, were the only historical events which have much connexion with the voyage. The triumph at Tidorè was of short duration, but Amboina was retained and much prized. Captain Fitz-herbert, writing in 1621, thus described the island: "*Amboyna* sitteth as queen between the isles of *Banda* and the *Moluccas*. She is beautified with the fruits of several factories, and dearly beloved of the *Dutch*."

If the establishment of peace removed the apprehensions of *one* casualty, it left the difficulties arising out of mercantile competition, which were somewhat formidable. The maritime efforts of the Portuguese, with regard to India, were on an immense scale.

From the voyage of Vasco da Gama in 1497 to the death of Emanuel I. in 1521, they despatched from Lisbon alone, as the vicomte de Santarem assures us, thirty-three fleets, composed of two hundred and twenty ships of war; and a fleet was despatched in every subsequent year till the date of this voyage. The fleet of 1604, which sailed on the 29th of April, carried out Martin Affonso de Castro, the viceroy, and consisted of five ships. Two carvels also sailed in the same year.

The Dutch, as mercantile rivals, were even more formidable than the Portuguese. The first fleet, of four ships, was despatched in 1595; the second, of eight ships, in 1598; etc. The union of certain Companies gave a fresh impulse to their proceedings. In 1602 they despatched fourteen ships and a yacht; and in December 1603, twelve ships. The latter fleet, commanded by admiral van der Hagen, or detachments of it, are frequently noticed in the journal.

The French, in point of time, claim precedence of the Dutch, Jean Parmentier of Dieppe having reached Sumatra in 1529—but the *Compagnie Française pour le commerce des Indes Orientales* was not established till 1664.

The services of Middleton in this voyage were promptly recognized: he was knighted at Greenwich on the 25th of May 1606. The Company, no doubt, were *more* than satisfied, as he had accomplished what they had not ventured to propose. Their views now became expanded, and they made application for letters in their favour, in the name of his Majesty, to the powers at Aden, Surat, and Calicut. The after career of sir Henry Middleton, I must not even touch on: it would require a volume to describe his adventures. I shall only observe that sir Dudley Digges styles him the "*thrice-worthy general, who laid the true foundation of our long-desired Cambaya trade.*" This eulogy was written in 1615.

The authenticity of the journal admits of no doubt. I have often tested its chronology, and have always found it correct. Its agreement with the Dutch journals, both as to dates and circumstances, is also in its favour. Moreover, as sir Henry Middleton left a daughter named Margaret *Burre*, it is probable that the publisher was his son-in-law, and that the permission to publish it was the consequence of that relationship. In editing the *text*, I have modernised the orthography and punctuation, and have restored the proper names to uniformity. In the *notes*, while adhering to the period in question, I have explained whatever seemed to require it. The *appendix*, I venture to hope, will interest many by the substantial information which it affords.

If I should undertake to edit another volume for the Hakluyt Society, it would be the voyage of Jean de Bethencourt to the Canary Islands in 1402, translated from the French, in its ancient guise, of Pierre Bontier and Jean le Verrier.

I am sensible, however, that more interest would be felt in any attempts to illustrate the progress of geographical discovery, and the state of political and commercial intercourse, with regard to India, the

Malaian archipelago, and those vast territories which we may now fairly call the *new world*—Australia and its islands. In this remark there may be a slight deviation from my proper course, to which I shall now return.

The historians of British India have been very imperfectly acquainted with the events which preceded the establishment of the continental factories, and it is a curious circumstance that Grant and Bruce, in adverting to those early voyages, should have relied on Anderson as much as if the volumes of Purchas were inaccessible, or had never been in existence.

I could not, after the evidence above stated, advise a reprint of those voyages as they appear in Purchas, but venture to suggest to aspirants in historical and geographical literature, as promising subjects, 1. A life of sir Thomas Smith, the first governor of the East-India Company; 2. An annotated edition of the voyage of sir James Lancaster in 1601; and 3. A compilation from Purchas, and other sources, of all the voyages and occurrences of note from 1606 to 1625. By the accomplishment of those objects the public would possess a mass of important and novel facts, and the future historian of India would be enabled to treat the defective portion of an interesting phase in its history with much more intelligence and exactness.

The India-House, the State-paper Office, the Chapel of the Rolls, the British Museum, and many other public repositories, would furnish various manuscript materials in illustration of those objects, and the list of authorities appended to this volume may serve to point out some of the books which should also be consulted. I shall now give the titles of three works which I had no occasion to quote, but cannot omit to recommend.

1. "Bibliothèque Asiatique et Africaine ou catalogue des ouvrages relatifs à l'Asie et à l'Afrique qui ont paru depuis la découverte de l'imprimerie jusqu'en 1700; par H. Ternaux-Compans. *Paris*, 1841." 8vo. pp. 6+348.

2. "Histoire du commerce entre le Levant et l'Europe depuis les croisades jusqu'à la fondation des colonies d'Amérique, par G. B. Depping, membre de la Société royale des antiquaires de France, *etc.* *Paris*, à l'Imprimerie royale. 1830." 8vo. 2 vols.

3. "Mémoire géographique, historique et scientifique sur l'Inde antérieurement au milieu du xie siècle de l'ère chrétienne, d'après les écrivains Arabes, Persans et Chinois, par M. Reinaud, membre de l'Institut de France, *etc.* *Paris*, Imprimerie nationale, 1849." 4to. pp. 8+400. *Avec une carte d'une partie de l'Asie, rédigée par M. d'Avezac.*

The first of the above works is an excellent specimen of bibliography; the second describes the modes in which the produce of India was formerly transported to Europe; and the third forms a learned and curious supplement to the standard works of Robertson and Vincent.

It shames me to observe the date at which the first sheets of this slim volume were consigned to the press, but as I can make no sufficient apology for omitting to resume the operations of editorship after some unavoidable suspensions, I must be content with the mental relief which it gives me to discharge the debt of honour so often vividly felt as due to the council of the Hakluyt Society.

I must now gratefully express my obligations to the right honourable sir George Grey, the Secretary of State for the home department, for the favour of permission to search for documents in the State-paper Office, and to the honourable the Court of Directors of the East-India Company, on the recommendation of the late sir Charles Malcolm, for the same favour with regard to the archives of the India-House; also to Mr. Rundall, of that establishment, for assisting me in my researches; and to Mr. Major, the able and active secretary of our society, for his prompt replies to my inquiries on all occasions.

BOLTON CORNEY.

The Terrace, Barnes.
28th March 1856.

DESCRIPTION OF THE PLATES.

Plate 1. (To face the title.) Chart of the Maluco Islands.—The outline from G. F. von Derfelden van Hinderstein, 1842.

Plate 2. (To face p. 1.) Wood-cut of the Red Dragon, captain Lancaster, in the Strait of Malacca, anno 1602.—From the Dutch collection of East-India voyages, 1645-6.

Plate 3. (To face p. 16.) Pictorial plan of Bantam, anno 1596. A. The tower; B. The water-gate; C. The river; D. The inland gate; E. THE ROYAL PALACE; F. The residence of the sabandar; G. The place of audience; H. The hill-gate; I. The mosque; K. The residence of *Andemoin;* L. The residence of the admiral; M. The residence of *Chenopate;* N. The residence of *Panjansiba;* O. The residence of *Satie Moluc;* P. The residence of the captain of Bantam; Q. The barrier-gate; R. The Dutch factory; S. The Chinese dwellings.—From the *Premier livre de l'histoire de la navigation avx Indes Orientales par les Hollandois,* etc. Amsterdam, 1609.

Plate 4. (To face p. 30.) The Dutch factory at Nera, one of the Banda Islands, anno 1599. The mode of weighing nutmegs and mace.—From *Le second livre, iovrnal ov comptoir,* etc. Amsterdam, 1609.

Plate 5. (To face p. 36.) Gammèlammè, the chief town in Ternatè, one of the Maluco Islands, anno 1599. A. The mosque; B. The house in which the king permitted the Dutch to reside; C. THE ROYAL PALACE, built of stone; D. Offices of the palace; E. The market place; F. The cloister of S. Paul, built by the Portuguese; G. The residence of the royal interpreter; H. A house built of stone by the Portuguese; I. A tower mounted with one cannon; K. A stake with the head of a captive; L. A gondola; M. A war caracoa; N. The approach to the town.—From *Le second livre,* etc. Amsterdam, 1609.

Plate 6. (To face p. 34.) Caracoas and fishing-boats. A caracoa of the king of Ternatè, carrying seven guns, javelins, etc.—rowed by slaves seated in *out-riggers* made of bamboo, and steered by paddles. Beneath is a small caracoa or galley, and various fishing boats.—From *Le second livre,* etc. Amsterdam, 1609.

THE Laſt Eaſt-Indian Voyage.

CONTAINING MVCH varietie of the State of the ſeuerall kingdomes where they haue traded: *with the Letters of three ſeuerall Kings to the Kings Maiestie of England,*

begun by one of the Voyage: ſince continued out of the faithfull obſeruations of them that are come home.

(·.·)

AT LONDON,

Printed by *T. P.* for *Walter Burre.*
1606.

TO THE READER.

Reader,

The *beginner of this relation following would no doubt, if he had lived, have himself set it out to thy good liking; but this I assure thee, that both his* [*part*], *and this continuation of it, is set forth with as much faithfulness as could be gathered out of the best observations of them that are come home. If I find it to thy liking, look shortly for an exact and large discourse written by master* Scott,[1] *chief factor at Bantam, ever since the first voyage—containing whatsoever hath happened since their first arrival there to trade in those parts. Read this; look for the other; and so farewell.*

W. B. [Walter Burre.]

1 "An *exact discovrse of the subtilties, fashions, pollicies, religion, and ceremonies of the East Indians,* etc. *Written by Edmund* Scott. 1606." 4to. A. to N. in fours.

PLATE 2.

The Red Dragon, Captain Lancaster, in the Strait of Malacca,
Anno 1602.

THE

LAST EAST-INDIAN VOYAGE;

CONTAINING MANY MEMORABLE MATTERS OF THE STATE OF THE COUNTRIES WHERE THEY HAVE TRADED.

MARCH THE 23RD, 1604.[1]

[SOVEREIGNS of maritime states, 1604.—England, Scotland, etc., James I. king; France, Henry IV. king; Spain and Portugal, Philip III. king—viceroy of India, Martin Affonso de Castro; Holland, Maurice de Nassau, prince of Orange, stadtholder.]

BEING provided of all things necessary for so long a voyage, with leave taken of the governor,[2] and others of the *committees,*[3] we departed from Gravesend the twenty-fifth of March,

[1] The fleet consisted of the four ships which had made the former voyage, namely: the Red Dragon, 600 tons, captain Henry Middleton, *general* or commodore, and captain David Middleton; the Hector, 500 tons, captain Christopher Colthurst, *lieutenant-general;* the Ascension, 260 tons, captain Roger Stiles; and the Susan, 240 tons, captain William Keeling. Captain Colthurst, captain Stiles, captain Keeling, master Robert Brown, and master Edward Highlord, formed the council of merchants. The complement of seamen is not stated.—*India-House Mss.*

[2] Sir Thomas Smith, knight—the first governor of the East-India company. He was also governor of the Muscovia company, and of other similar associations. In 1604 he went on an embassy to Russia. He died in 1625. Sir Thomas enclosed an invoice of the cash and merchandise on board the four ships in a farewell letter to his *loving friend* captain Keeling, dated *In Gravesend, the 25th of March* 1604.—Stow; *Registrum Roffense; India-House Mss.*; etc.

[3] The committee, as appointed by the first charter, consisted of the governor, a deputy-governor, and twenty-four other members. Each member of it was also styled a *committee.*—*Charters* E. I. C.

being Sunday at night,[4] and the Tuesday following came to the Downs, where the general, before we came to an anchor, gave order to the purser to call the company, and take their names—which being done, there was found forty men lacking of the *copelment* [complement] of our ship, so that we were forced thereby to come to anchor to tarry for them. The general gave order presently[5] the pinnace should be manned, and sent the master, with his brother and the purser, for better despatch, to Sandwich; where they escaped very near drowning. The Ascension's pinnace likewise put off to set their pilot a-land, and so was cast away; which, when the general heard of, he was exceeding angry with captain Stiles, that he would offer to go a-land at such a time without his order. The last of March, the master, captain Middleton, and the master's mate, came aboard.

The first of April we weighed anchor in the Downs, and, thwart Dover,[6] we found our men in ketches ready to come aboard: we took them all into our ship, being twenty-eight men, which was far short of that number we expected. But, howsoever, the general was determined to proceed, although he lacked forty men, rather than lose the benefit of so fair a wind. So the same day, off Beachy [Beachy-Head], the general gave order to the boatswain to take new muster of our men; and he found we had twenty more than our *copelment* aboard the admiral; and, tarrying to speak with the rest of the ships, we hailed them one after another, and found

4 The departure on *Sunday* may have been a piece of contrivance. Seamen were rather superstitious, and commonly held it "good to begin the voyage on Sundaies."—Sir H. Manwayring.

5 Here, and elsewhere in the text, *presently* appears to be used in the sense of *forthwith*—as in Shakspere:

> "These likelihoods confirm her flight from hence:
> Therefore, I pray you, stand not to discourse,
> But mount you *presently*."

6 The former edition has "*twarth* Dover". It must be an error of the press. I conclude the author wrote *thwart* = *abreast of* Dover.

they had every ship more than their *copelment*—the cause of which error could not be imagined, without foul weather caused them to hide themselves at such time of general muster; or else, that some of them, misdoubting they should be set on land, played least in sight: but, howsoever, this overplus of men was as grievous to the general as the lack he had afore. To see how he had been deluded to come to anchor with a fair wind for lack of men, and now of force must put into some place to set them again a-land! So the general gave order to the master he should have a care he did not pass Plymouth that night, for that he was minded[7] to put in there to discharge those men. So the next day morning at day-break we were ready, with tacks aboard,[8] to stand into the sound of Plymouth, and stood in a good while till such time as it began to be gusty weather, and the wind to *souther* upon us, so that we were enforced against the general's liking to proceed on our voyage, steering alongst the land with much wind[9]—and in the afternoon we lost sight of England; and so continuing our course with a fair wind, upon Thursday, being the sixth day of April, we were thwart Cape Finisterre, and the seventh day off *the Rock* [Cape Roca]; and upon Easter-day, being the eighth day, off Cape Saint Vincent, with the wind large,[10] and fair weather; and continuing our course till the fifteenth, we came to the Canaries—where, in the calms, trial was made to take in the Hector's boat, but she could not stow her by reason she was both too long and too broad, which if she could have

7 *Minded*, as an adjective, is commonly interpreted by *disposed*. Here, and in various instances, it has the force of *resolved*.

8 When a ship has her sails trimmed very obliquely to the wind, she is said to be *close-hauled*, or to have her *tacks aboard*.—W. Falconer.

9 I shall now commence with the *Discourse* of Thomas Clayborne, as we have it in the *briefe extract* made by Purchas: *The Ascension*. "The second day of April 1604, being Monday, about twelve of the clock, we had sight of the Lizard."—T. Clayborne.

10 When a ship has the wind very favourable, or somewhat abaft the beam, she is said to have the *wind large*.—W. Falconer.

done the general was minded not to touch in any place till he doubled the Cape [of Good Hope]. So that was the principal cause he went to the Islands of Cape Verde: so the same night we departed from the Canaries, and directed our course for Maio, one of the foresaid islands.[11]

The twenty-second day we had sight of Boa-Vista.[12] The twenty-fourth day we anchored at Maio, upon the south-west side, where the general with the rest of the captains and merchants went a-land to seek fresh water; but there was none to be found but a small well, which would yield scarce a hogshead a day. Presently after our landing there came to our general a *Portingal*[13] that had wounded one of his fellows, desiring to save his life, and upon that condition he would give him all the wealth he had, which was some five hundred dried goats. The general would give no ear to him, nor his request, for that he would give no occasion of offence to them of the island; yet by entreaty of the vice-admiral, and the other captains, he was contented to take his goats and him aboard—which presently was effected. Also the same afternoon there came two Portingals more of the island to our general, who came very kindly unto him and bade him welcome. So after some discourse the general desired them that for his money he might buy some live goats of them for the refreshing of his men. They presently made

[11] The Cape Verde Islands, from the peculiarity of their position, have been visited by the most eminent early navigators. Maio, one of the group, was noted for its salt. In the event of a separation of the fleet by foul weather, it was the appointed place of rendezvous.—Capt. Davis; *Instructions*, § 4.

[12] *The Ascension.* "The three-and-twentieth day [of April], west-south-west to the westward, two-and-twenty leagues, latitude fifteen degrees and five minutes; and this day we fell with the westermost part of S. Iago, being west-by-north six leagues, and at five of the clock we stood to the eastward for Maio, the wind at north."—T. Clayborne.

[13] *Portingal*, in lieu of Portugal, occurs only once; in lieu of Portuguese, *very* frequently. In the former edition it is variously spelt: 1. Portingal; 2. Portingale; 3. Portingall. I have adopted the first mode.

answer again they would sell none, but that we might kill as many as we would, and nobody would be offended thereat; and so presently they went with the general and showed him how we should enclose them, and so set our dogs upon them; and having killed half-a-dozen of goats they took their leave in friendly manner for that night, promising in the morning to return and bring their dogs with them, and to help us to so many goats as we would desire.[14] So the general, with all the rest, came presently aboard.[15]

The next day the general would not go a-land, but sent captain Stiles, captain Keeling, and captain Middleton, with express order to keep their people from straggling; and when all their company were landed, captain Stiles called them all together, giving them warning to keep company together, and not range one from the other; which speech was reiterated again by master Durham, saying that whosoever was found straggling should be severely punished, and therefore willed them all to take good heed. And so, after this warning given, they marched up into the country to kill some goats, where they met with two *Portugals*,[16] which did assist them in all *the* [their] might. In the meanwhile they were at their sport a-land, the general with the rest were busy in stowing the Hector's long boat, for that he was minded to go to sea so soon as they had done; but they could not stow her with-

[14] *Dried goats*, etc.—I can only give the following explanation: when sir Francis Drake was at the Cape Verde Islands, a Portuguese pilot informed him "that vpon one of those islands, called Mayo, there was great store of dryed *cabritas* [she-kids], which a few inhabitants there dwelling did yeerely make ready for such of the kings ships as did there touch, beeing bound for his countrey of Brasile or elsewhere."—Hakluyt.

[15] *The Ascension.* "The four-and-twentieth day [of April] we fell with Maio, and stood to the southward of the island, and came to anchor at fifteen fathoms, one point north-west-and-by-north, and the other east-south-east."—T. Clayborne.

[16] *Portugal*, in lieu of Portuguese, occurs frequently—chiefly as a substantive. It is variously spelt; and, to dispense with notes on orthographical matters, I shall give a table of proper names.

out cutting off her stem and part of her bows, which, seeing no other way, was presently effected. And so, drawing towards night, our land-men repaired aboard with some few goats they had killed; and after supper, the wind coming off the land, the general gave order to the master to weigh [anchor], and that a warning-piece might be shot off—and so presently the cable was brought to capstan, and our ship was presently loose; but before we had up our anchor, captain Stiles sent word one of their merchants was missing: so that we came presently to anchor again, and did ride till day. He that lost himself was the party [master Durham] which was so careful to give other men warning, which took none himself. Day no sooner appearing but the general sent captain Stiles, with at least one hundred and fifty men, to seek for him;[17] and if it were possible to speak with some of the Portugals, but all that day was spent in vain, and no news of him; so the general would spend no longer time there, but left him to learn the language![18] So the sixteenth of May we passed the line,[19] where many of our men fell sick of the scurvy, calenture, bloody flux, and the worms; being left to the mercy of God, and a small quantity of lemon-juice[20] every morning: our physician, shipped for that purpose,

[17] *The Ascension.* "The five-and-twentieth day [of April] we landed, and lost one of our merchants, who was taken by the people of the island. The six-and-twentieth day, in the morning, we landed an hundred men to see if we could get our merchant again, but could not come near any of the people of the island; so we left him behind us, and this night, about nine of the clock, we set sail, the wind at north."—T. Clayborne.

[18] An allusion, I conceive, to the letter of queen Elizabeth to the *mighty king* of Acheen, in which she requests his majesty to permit captain Lancaster to leave certain factors there, to *learn the language*.—Purchas.

[19] *The Ascension.* "The sixteenth day of May, latitude fifteen minutes, and this day we passed the equinoctial."—T. Clayborne.

[20] The deficiency of *lemon-juice* was an unfortunate oversight. Captain Lancaster had proved its importance. "The reason why the generals men stood better in health then the men of other ships, was this: he brought to sea with him certaine bottles of the iuice of limons—by this meanes the generall cured many of his men, and preserued the rest."—Purchas.

being as unwilling as ignorant in anything that might help them—a great oversight in the company, and no doubt will be better looked to hereafter.

And to our *proceeding* voyage: the thirteenth day of July, being Friday, we had sight of Cape Boa Esperança[21] [the Cape of Good Hope]. The wind at south-west, a gentle gale, the general commanded the tacks aboard, intending to go about the Cape, but our sick men cried out most lamentably, for at that present there were sick of the scurvy at the least eighty men in our ship, not one able to help the other, who made a petition to the general, most humbly entreating him for God's sake to save their lives, and to put in for *Saldania*,[22] otherways they were but dead men. The general perusing their pitiful complaint, and looking out of his cabin door, where did attend a swarm of lame and weak diseased cripples, who beholding this lamentable sight extended his compassion towards them, and granted their requests.[23] That night the wind came up at the south, and continued till the seventeenth day before we could get into the road.[24] The next morning, being Wednesday, the general went on land, with provision to set up tents; and a little way from our landing-place, the negroes had their houses—which were no other than a few

[21] *The Ascension.* "The thirteenth of July, in the forenoon, we had sight of Cape Boa Esperança, being off us fifteen leagues."—T. Clayborne.

[22] *Saldania. Agoada de Saldanha*, or Saldanha watering-place, was so named by Antonio de Saldanha, who went to India in 1503. The Saldanha Bay of modern geographers is a misnomer. *The Saldanha Bay of De Barros, and of the early English and Dutch navigators, is our Table Bay.* Captain Raymond put in here in 1591; captain Houtman in 1598; captain Lancaster in 1601; and sir Edward Michelborne in 1605.—De Barros; Hakluyt; Purchas; etc.

[23] The general was authorised to refresh at *St. Lawrence*, now called Madagascar, but "not at *Saldania* in anywise." The probable reason for this injunction appears in a subsequent note.—*Instructions*, § 6.

[24] *The Ascension.* "The seventeenth day we came to anchor in the road of Saldanha, having sixty men sick of the scurvy; but, God be praised, they all recovered health before we went from hence."—T. Clayborne.

crooked sticks set in the ground, and mats cast over them—and they had great store of cattle, both beeves and sheep, grazing *fair by* them.[25] Our general and the captains went to barter with them for small pieces of iron, and bought some twelve sheep, and more would have sold us till that they saw us begin to set up our tents, which as it seemed was to their disliking, for that, incontinent, they pulled down their houses and made them fast upon their beasts' backs, and did drive away; yet all means possible was sought to draw them to sell us more, but in no case they would abide any longer with us, but drove away with all the speed they might. It lay in the general's power to have taken them all from them, as some counselled him to do, but he in no case would give ear thereunto, but let them depart, not doubting but that they would return again, seeing we offered them no wrong when it was in our powers to dispossess them of all their cattle.[26]

The nineteenth day we got our sick men on land, and the twentieth our boats were sent to the island, where we found such infinite number of seals that it was admirable to behold! all the sea-shore lies over-spread with them, some sleeping, some travelling into the island, and some to the seaward; besides all the rocks which lie a pretty distance off, so full as they can hold—thousands at a time going and as many coming out: there be many of them as big as any bear, and as terrible to behold. And up towards the middle of the island there be infinite numbers of fowls called penguins, pelicans, and cormorants. The penguins be as big as our greatest capons we have in England; they have no wings,

[25] *Fair by* must mean *conveniently near*. The expression occurs about ten times, and seems always to have the same import.

[26] The instructions given to the general respecting intercourse with the natives of the places at which the fleet might touch for refreshment, are sensible and humane. He was to keep *warlike guard* on shore; to prohibit straggling; to exhort to moderation of diet; to appoint certain persons as purveyors; and to admonish his men to behave towards the natives *peaceably and civilly*.—*Instructions*, § 5.

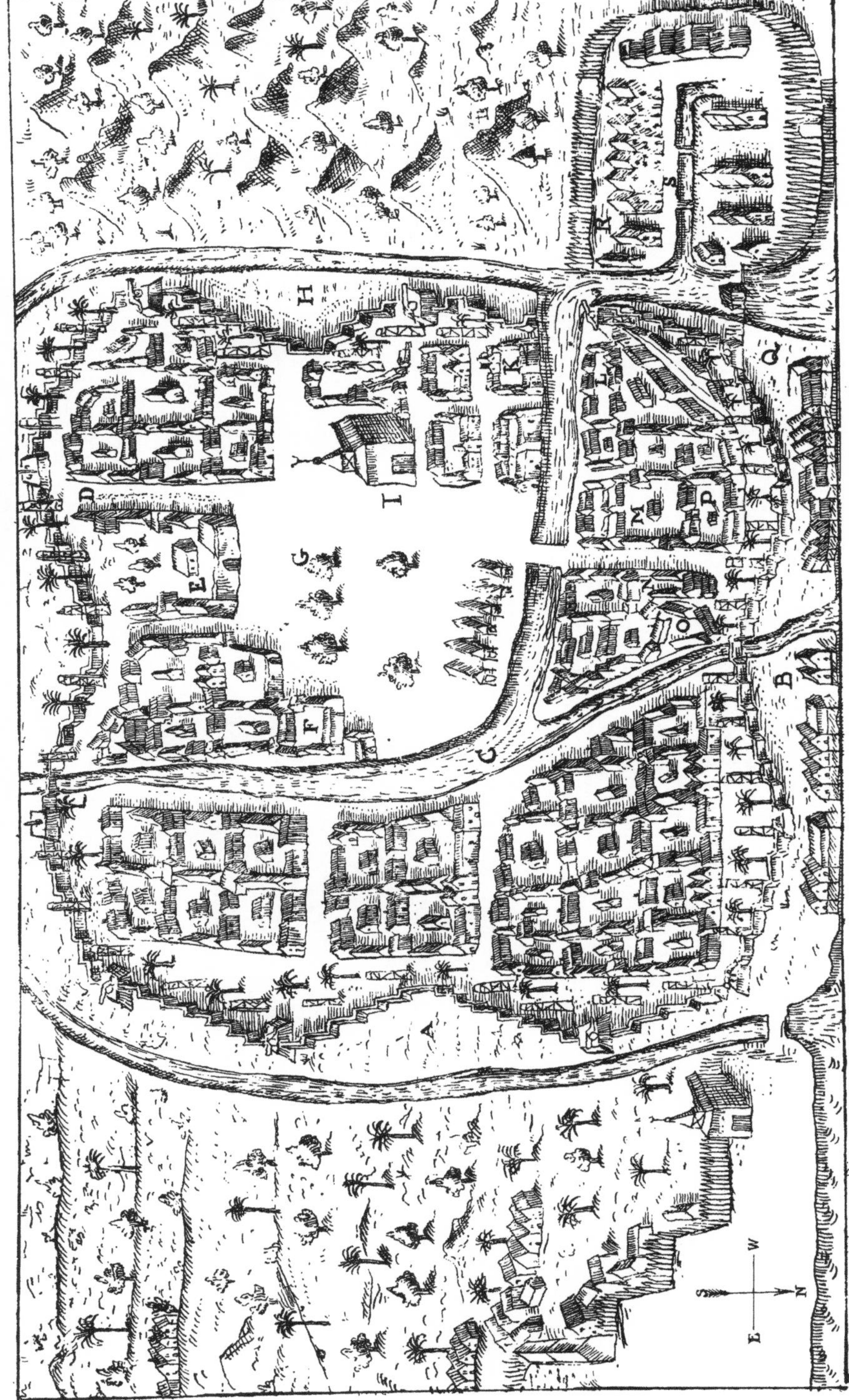

nor cannot fly, but you may drive them by thousands in a flock whither you will. They be exceeding fat, but their flesh is very rank, for that they live upon fish: there be so many of them upon this small island, which is not above five miles about, to lade a ship of fifty tons withal.[27]

Upon Sunday, the twenty-third, the first man that died out of our ship. Upon Monday morning the general went into the country to buy fresh victuals, but the people of the country, seeing so many in company, fled. But the general caused all the company to make a stand, and then sent four to them with a bottle of wine and victuals, with a tabor and a pipe. They seeing no more in company came to them, and did eat, drink, and dance with them; so they, seeing with what kindness they were used, took heart unto them, and came along with our general to our tents; where they had many toys bestowed upon them, as pins, points, beads, and branches[28]—and so they returned all very well pleased, making signs to return the next day with cattle; but foul weather prevented them for three days. The fourth day after, being the twenty-sixth, they brought us forty-four sheep, and the next day twenty-three sheep and two kine, and the next day fifteen sheep and one bullock, and the thirtieth day we bought one-hundred-and-twenty sheep and six beeves, the next day nine sheep and three beeves, and the second of August three sheep.[29]

The third of August the general went in his pinnace, and other boats with him, to kill whales, for all the bay is full of

27 This island lies seven miles north-north-west of Cape Town. It was afterwards called *Penguin Island*, but now appears in our charts as *Robben Island*—from the Dutch word *rob*=a seal.—Lieut. Vidal; etc.

28 *Points* and *branches*. *Points*, frequently noticed by our early dramatic writers, were *tagged laces*. *Branches* may be a misprint for *brooches*, or it may mean *artificial flowers*.—Nares; etc.

29 The current prices are not reported. When captain Raymond was here in 1591, as before noticed, the price of an ox was two knives, and of a sheep, one knife. We read, in the margin of the narrative, "*Oxen and sheepe dog-cheape!*"—Hakluyt.

them. They struck divers with harping-irons,[30] and especially they in the Susan's pinnace, struck their harping-iron into one of them very sure, and veered their boat a good scope from her. She, feeling herself wounded, towed the boat for the space of half-an-hour up and down the bay with such swiftness, that the men were fain to go all of them and sit in the stern, and let the whale tow them, which was with such swiftness that she seemed to fly; but in the end they were enforced to cut their rope, to keep their boat from sinking, they were carried so swiftly through the sea. The next that struck one was in the general's pinnace, and there were two of them together, and their fortune was to strike a young one which played *like reakes*[31] as the first did, and continued for a good time; and then they hauled up the boat somewhat near, and wounded her in divers places with javelins. The great whale, all this time, would not depart from the little one, although it had received many wounds, but stood to the last to fight it out against all our boats—sometimes giving one boat a blow, and sometimes another, and would come under our boats, and lift them almost out of the water! She bestowed one bang on the general's pinnace that split all the timbers and boards, so that he was fain to take another boat to save himself, for she was presently full of water—yet, with much ado, they saved the pinnace, and brought her on land, where it cost all our carpenters three days' work to repair her. And when the young whale began to be weary, the old one would take the young upon his back, and carry him; but the old one seeing that would not prevail against us,

30 The term *harping-iron* was formerly used instead of *harpoon*. The poet Waller may be cited in proof. In his picturesque account of a whale-fight at the Burmudas, we read:

> "The boat which on the first assault did go,
> Struck with a *harping-iron* the younger foe."

31 *Played like reakes* = played the same tricks. The word *reakes* occurs in the French *Dictionarie* of Randle Cotgrave, London, 1611. v. *Degonder*.—J. O. Halliwell.

would leave his carriage,[32] and betake himself to his fight, which was to cast his tail out of the water, and to strike so valiantly, that if he had taken any of our boats with one of these blows he would have split it all to pieces. It was very good sport to stand and look on, but very dangerous to them in the boats. To conclude of this matter, the young whale could not be killed till the sun-set; the old one never forsaking her whilst it had any life.[33] So after it was dead we towed it to our landing-place, and at high water hauled it so high as we could. The occasion why we killed this whale was for lack of oil for our lamps, for in all the ships we had great lack. The oil was put in very bad *caske*,[34] and leaked out; but whereas, we hoped to have had oil enough out of this whale to have served all our turns, it did scarce yield four gallons, it was so young and lean.

The eighth day the general sent a dozen of our men to buy fresh victuals, for that we had not any left; so they were out all day, and brought home but two sheep. At their return, whieh was late, the general demanded of the purser of the Hector, which was chief purveyor, what was the occasion they staid out so long, and that they brought no more cattle: he answered, that the people had sold them good store of cattle, which he had paid for, but being so few of our men in company, and they weaponless, they would abuse them in snatching their iron from them, and not to suffer them to drive the cattle away they paid for. The general,

32 *Carriage* is evidently used as the synonym of *burden*. It is now obsolete in that sense. It occurs, however, in Spenser and in Shakspere.

33 The adventure so graphically narrated in this paragraph, may be the origin of our southern whale-fishery. It is certain, at least, that the accounts of previous voyages, whether by the English or Dutch, give no other hint on this subject; but, about six years afterwards, the bay had become noted for a *small sort of whales*, and it was visited by two Dutch ships for the purpose of making *train oil of seals*.—Purchas.

34 *Caske* for *casks*. I shall justify this apparent erratum by a quotation: "Some man might ask me how we came to have so many empty *caske* in less than two months."—Sir R. Hawkins.

seeing how they used him, thought by policy to go beyond them;[35] and this it was: he himself, with one-hundred-and-twenty men in his company, would go by night and lie in ambush in a wood near the place where our men did barter with them, and when it was fair day the purveyor and his crew should come, as [at] other times, and bargain with them for so many as they would sell; and when they had sufficient, to make a sign, and then the general and his company should come out of their lodgings, and drive them away. This matter was put in practice this night, and the general, three hours before day, departed from the tents, and had imbosked himself[36] and all his followers to their own contents; only three fellows of captain Stiles his company, to taste of a bottle of wine they carried for their captain, and in the mean while they were drinking, they had lost sight of their general and all his company, and took a contrary way, never staying till they came to the houses of the negroes. They, seeing three men armed to come to their houses, began to suspect some false measures: these fellows, seeing they had mistaken themselves, retired back to the woods, and, in sight of the Indians, hid themselves in the bushes. At that time, the sun being up, half-an-hour after these fellows had hid themselves, came our weaponless merchants from the tents, and began to barter with them for two or three sheep, which of purpose they had sent down to our people to keep them busy while they were getting their herds of cattle to run away; which our merchants perceiving, they presently, unarmed as they were, went amongst them, and sent word by one of them

35 The *policy* was questionable. Captain Lancaster, in similar circumstances, acted more advisedly. He appointed half-a-dozen persons to barter with the natives, and had some thirty men within sight, armed with muskets and pikes, in constant readiness—*what occasion soever should befall.* "I take this to be the cause," says the anonymous journalist of the voyage, "why we lived in so great friendship and amity with them."—Purchas.

36 To *imbosk*, in an active sense, is of rare occurrence; but the author needs no apology. The word is very appositely introduced.

to the general to come away with all his people, for that he and all his company were discovered. So that the general was enforced to break out of his ambushment to rescue his men, which were amongst them without weapons; but before he could come to their rescue, they had wounded one of our men with four darts sticking in his body, which being done they betook them to their heels, and all the cattle before them, as fast as they could drive to the mountains.[37] Our men, as then having the reins in their own hands, pursued after them in such scattering manner, that if the people of the country had been men of any resolution they might have cut off most of them. The general caused a trumpet to sound a retreat, but could not cause them to leave their chace; and whilst that he was taking order[38] to send the hurt man to the tents, he was half-a-mile from the nearest of our men, and not past five men in his company: so he, and those men in his company, were fain to run to overtake some of them which were before—that in the end they were a dozen in his company. Yet the general took it grievous to see his men scattered over all the plain, and scarce three of them together in a company, which if the people of the country had joined together, and set upon them being so scattered, they had cut most of them off, which thing the general greatly doubted.[39] Yet, God be thanked, it sorted better; for some of our men overtook some of the negroes at the foot of the mountain, and drave

[37] This was a fortunate escape. Houtman, only six years before, had mournful proof of the treachery of the natives. The event is thus described by an eye-witness, captain John Davis: "there came great troops of them to us, bringing very much cattle with them, and in the time of bartering, suddenly taking their advantage, they set upon us, and slew thirteen of our people with *hand darts* [assegais], which at four pikes length could not offend."—Purchas.

[38] To *take order*, which thrice occurs, means to *take measures*—as in this extract: "I [the admiral] *took order* for victuals for the soldiers on land to be brought to Puntall."—Viscount Wimbledon.

[39] To *doubt* is here used in the sense of to *fear;* and it seems to bear that sense on every other occasion in the course of this narrative.

them away from some of their cattle, and made a stand by them till more of their company came up, and so returned homewards with a hundred kine and calves, which was welcome to our sick men.

But in our absence from our tents, captain Colthurst, with the master [Sander Cole] and such as were left, being very doubtful all was not well with us, thought it best to send our pinnace to the bottom of the bay to help us if we stood in need; but master Cole, being over-bold in his pinnace to go ashore, both he and the boat were cast away, and two more, that presumed of their swimming, were drowned.[40] The rest escaped very hardly; came running naked along the sands to us-wards; and there certified the general of all that happened, which was but sorrowful news to him. The next day the general sent sufficient store of men to march by land to the place where the boat was cast away, and found her dry upon the strand, split and full of sand; but with much trouble she was freed, and sent aboard. Also we found master Cole upon the strand, and brought him to our tents and buried him.[41]

This night, and the next after, our sentinels had spied the country people lurking about our tents, so that alarum[42] was given, and they fled. Upon the fourteenth of August we departed all aboard our ships, where we rode till the nineteenth, the wind not serving to carry us out, which then served our turns;[43] we put to sea, and stood to the west-

40 *The Ascension.* "Saldanha is in latitude thirty-three degrees, fifty-six minutes, or thirty-four degrees. Here master Cole was drowned, being master of the Hector, our vice-admiral; and here we staid five weeks wanting a day."—T. Clayborne.

41 Sander Cole was master of the Hector in the former voyage. He is described, in the printed account of that voyage, as *an honest and a good man*—so I record the words as the best of epitaphs.—Purchas.

42 The former edition has *alarome.* The word was thus defined: "*Alarum.* An out-cry signifying, To your arms."—*English Expositor.*

43 *The Ascension.* "The twentieth day of August, being Monday, we weighed and set sail out of the road of Saldanha, the wind southerly, and we stood to the westward."—T. Clayborne.

ward, and the twenty-fifth day we doubled the Cape of Good Hope, with very favorable winds till the fifth of September, and after that time we met with the wind scarce, and now and then calms; and here began the scurvy to grow amongst our men, and every day did the disease increase.[44] Here might somewhat be said of the ignorance and uncharitableness of him that was shipped for our physician, as a caveat to them that shall go hereafter to be better provided; but for two respccts I forbear—the one in regard of his other calling, but chiefly for that he is since dead in the voyage, where, for my part, I wish his faults may be buried with him.[45]

The nineteenth of December we had sight of Engano, an island lying near Sumatra;[46] the twentieth we had sight of Sumatra; the twenty-first we anchored within the islands, where we were put to great trouble to have up our yards and get up our anchors. Our men were exceeding weak; we were fain to send men out of our ship to help the rest, and so with much ado we came to Bantam road. The occasion why we first anchored was, because the Ascension shot off a piece of ordnance within night, which was contrary to our articles;[47] we, doubting she was in some great distress, came suddenly to an anchor to tarry to know what was the matter, which proved to be nothing but that their gunner was dead and thrown overboard, and had that piece for a

44 The scurvy is clearly indicated in the *Roteiro* of the voyage of Vasco da Gama in 1497; and it is the earliest notice of it which I can call to memory. At the period now in question, it prevailed to a frightful extent.—*Roteiro;* Jean Mocquet; Sir R. Hawkins; etc.

45 After refreshing, the general was to shape his course *direct* for Bantam; and as he had put into Saldanha Bay contrary to *express order*, and staid there five weeks, he crossed the Indian Ocean without touching at Madagascar.—*Instructions*, § 7.

46 Ships bound for the Sunda Strait in the north-west monsoon, which prevails from October to March, endeavour to make the Island of Engano —so the general had an excellent land-fall.—J. Horsburgh.

47 *Articles.* A code of instructions issued by a naval commander, and divided into *articles;* whence the name.—Viscount Wimbledon.

farewell; which folly of theirs put us to great trouble, causing us to anchor in the sea in twenty-five fathoms, then winds all westerly, which brought in a great seagate,[48] that the next day morning we had much ado to get up our anchor; and as for the other ships, they were not able to weigh without our helps, which we sent them; and so, with very much trouble, we got us all under sail, steering away east-and-by-north and east-north-east till we came to anchor between the island and the main, at the entrance of Bantam Bay, in seven fathoms, sandy ground.[49]

This night [the twenty-second] at seven a-clock, came a Hollands boat aboard us from Bantam, sent by a general of twelve ships[50] which came there two days before us; in which boat came the vice-admiral of the fleet, with refreshing from shore, presenting it to our general, with offer of any kindness they could do us, which afterwards they effected towards us in sending their boats to fetch us water—many other courtesies besides, we of ourselves not able to do the same, our weakness being so great.[51] This fleet had passed along the coast from Moçambique to Ceylon, and had taken

48 *Seagate* means the *swell of the sea.* Example: "The best ground [for ships] to ride in, is—where they may ride land-locked, so as that the *sea-gate* can have no power against them."—Sir H. Manwayring.

49 Bantam, situated at the north-west extremity of Java, was a principal mart for pepper; and frequented, as such, by Arabs, Guzerats, Chinese, etc. A plan of the town, as it existed in 1596, is added to this edition of the voyage. The Dutch reached Bantam in that year. The English factory was established by captain Lancaster in December 1602. —Edmund Scott; etc.

50 This fleet doubled the Cape on the first of June 1604, N.S.—The commander-in-chief was Etienne van der Hagen; the vice-admiral, Corneille Sebastiaanz. The ships were armed, and well manned; and the total burden was 5550 tons. The proceedings of this fleet, as stated in the *Recueil des Voiages* edited by C. de Renneville, shall be noticed in summaries or extracts—headed *The Dutch fleet*, and signed C. de Renneville.

51 *The Dutch fleet.* "Le 31 [de Décembre 1604. N.S.] la flotte mouilla l'ancre à la rade de Bantam.—Le 2 de Janvier 1605, quatre vaisseaux Anglais, fort faibles d'équipages, mouillèrent aussi à la rade de Bantam, commandés par l'amiral *Middelton.*—C. de Renneville.

divers ships and burned a carack, and afterwards came hither with all their men in good health.[52] An hour after their coming aboard of the Hollanders, came a prāu,[53] or a canoe, from Bantam, with master Scott and others of our men left there the last voyage, by whom the general knew the estate of their business.[54]

The twenty-third at two a-clock we came to anchor in Bantam road,[55] and saluted the town and Hollanders with most of our ordnance, and were answered again with the like from all the Hollanders. The twenty-fourth day our vice-admiral was sent unto the king to excuse the general's not coming a-land, for that he was not well. This day, being the twenty-fourth, came in two sail of Hollands fleet, a ship and a pinnace; the same day one of the thieves that had set our house on fire was stabbed to death,[56] according to the order of the country. The twenty-sixth day the general gave new articles to all the ships, wherein every man was absolutely forbidden to buy any spice,[57] and divers other articles for the good demeanour of his men, which here I omit to write. The twenty-seventh, twenty-eighth, and the twenty-

52 *The Dutch fleet.* Our author, in one particular, was misinformed. The fleet sailed *direct* from Moçambique to Goa; thence to Cananor, Calicut, Cochin, Colombo, etc.—C. de Renneville.

53 The former edition has *prawe.* Some write *proa;* others, *prahu.* It is a Malay word, and I therefore give it as above.—W. Marsden.

54 *Bantam.* "The two-and-twentieth day of December, towards evening, we descried our ships coming into the road, to all our extraordinary great joy; but when we came aboard of our admiral, and saw their weakness, also hearing of the weakness of the other three ships, it grieved us much."—E. Scott.

55 *The Ascension.* "The three-and-twentieth of December, being Sunday, we came to anchor in Bantam road, where we found six Holland ships, and three or four pinnaces."—T. Clayborne.

56 The former edition has *stopped to death.* It is a misprint. The offender was one *Uniete,* a Chinese; and the *kris,* or poniard, was the usual instrument of execution.—E. Scott.

57 The prohibition to buy spice extended to persons of all ranks and ratings; but it may not have been inserted in the *articles* till the arrival of the fleet at Bantam.—*Instructions,* § 13.

ninth, nothing happened worth writing. The thirtieth day the general of the Hollanders and most part of the principal of his fleet dined aboard with our general. The thirty-first our general went on land, with a letter from our king's majesty, and a present to the king of Bantam,[58] which he delivered him, and were very acceptably received—the king but thirteen years of age and governed by a protector.

The third day [of January 1605] we had order to rummage[59] our hold to take provision of water and merchants' goods, for that we were appointed, and the Ascension, to go for the Malucos, and the other ships to take in their lading of pepper, and to go home;[60] likewise this day we took in divers fardels of merchandise,[61] and so continued taking in water and merchandise till the eighth day, and then our general came aboard, and appointed such men as should go along with him to the Malucos, amongst which number master Taverner was removed from the Susan to the Ascension; we continued busy in taking in of merchandise and victuals of the Hector and the Susan, till the fifteenth day we made an end of taking

58 This royal letter is printed in the *Appendix*. The presents were, "one fair basin and ewer, two fair standing cups, all parcel-gilt, one gilt spoon, and six muskets with their furniture."—E. Scott.

59 To *rummage*, as a sea-term, seems to have meant *giving room* by improved stowage. It is capriciously spelt—as, *ruming*, *romeging*, *roomeging*, *romaging*, etc.—Capt. Smith; etc.

60 Various circumstances here require explanation. The general had directions to send home two ships from Bantam, and to proceed to Banda with the others—the choice of the ships for the latter service being left to himself and the principal factors. A council was therefore held, and it was resolved that the Red Dragon and the Ascension were the fittest for the voyage to Banda, and that the Hector and the Susan should return to England. In consequence of this decision, captain Colthurst was removed to the Ascension; captain Keeling promoted to the Hector, on the decease of captain Stiles; and master Edward Highlord appointed to the Susan, vice Keeling.—*Instructions*, § 12, 26; E. Scott.

61 The factory must have been crowded with merchandise, about a thousand *fardels* of calicos and pintados, and many other articles, having been taken in a Portuguese carack by captain Lancaster, in the Strait of Malacca, in October 1602.—Purchas; C. de Renneville.

in of merchandise. This day our purser William Griffen and master Foster died, both of the flux.[62]

The sixteenth day our general departed from Bantam, and came aboard to proceed on his voyage to the Malucos; this night died Henry Dewbrey of the flux; also the same day master Surfflict was appointed to go home in the Hector, to the great contenting of all in our ship:[63] likewise one of our master's mates, master Smith, was appointed for master's mate in the Hector. The seventeenth day died of the flux William Lewed, John Jenkens, and Samuel Porter. The eighteenth day the general having despatched his letters, went aboard the Hector and the Susan, and took leave of them;[64] and after dinner weighed, and stood to the sea-ward till night, and then anchored in eight fathoms of water. The nineteenth in the morning we weighed again, and proceeded with a fair wind till six a-clock at night, and then came to anchor in fourteen fathoms, oozy ground, fair by a small island. The twentieth, by break of day, we weighed, and stealing along[65] the land with a fair wind; this day died Henry Stiles our master carpenter, and James Varnam, and John Iberson, all of the flux. The twenty-first and twenty-second

62 The former edition has *flixe*, and so the word is spelt in the *Alvearie* of J. Barret, London, 1580. It is the prevailing complaint in Java, for which reason the natives, as an antidote, eat much *bumbu* or curry-stuff.—E. Scott; W. Marsden.

63 Master Surfflict left England on board the Red Dragon, as *doctor of physic* and *preacher*. He is the person on whose incompetence, in the former capacity, the author of this narrative has before twice animadverted. He died on his way home.—E. Scott.

64 *The Ascension.* "The eighteenth day of January [1605], we set sail out of Bantam road, with the Dragon and the Ascension; but they parted at Amboina. The general went with the Dragon to the Malucos, and the Ascension, whereof M. Colthurst was captain, for Banda; and the Hector and the Susan laded pepper at Bantam, and set sail from thence about the middle of February."—T. Clayborne *alias* S. Purchas.

65 *Stealing along.* The context requires *stole along*. It means that the ships made more progress than might be expected. *How she steals along!* is a phrase which I have heard on the Thames.

days we held on our course, with *blusting* rainy weather; the twenty-second day died of the flux James Hope; the twenty-fourth day in the morning we fell with[66] the shoals which lie off the east-north-east part of Java;[67] this day died John Leay and Robert Whitthers of the flux. January the twenty-fifth we held on our course with very much wind and rain; at night one of our men leaped over-board, having the calenture, and three more died of the flux—their names were William Bellidine, William Pooter, Gideon Marten, and Robert Vennes.

The twenty-sixth day steering our course with a fair wind, suspecting no danger, upon a sudden we saw the ground under the ship; heaving over the lead, we had but four fathoms water: this night died of the flux George Johnes, and Francis Buckman, and Gilbert Mesterson. The twenty-seventh day in the morning we steered away east-and-by-south; we came into shoal-water which lieth to the southward of *Ruinata*,[68] so that we were fain to stand south-and-by-west and south to get clear of the shoals, till noon, and then we came into deep water; and so bearing up[69] we steered east-and-by-south, and by and by we were in five fathoms, so that we stood to the southward some three leagues, and then held on our former course. This day died of the flux Robert

66 *Fell with* is equivalent to *fell in with*—as in this extract: "We passed in sight of the Burlings, and the Rock, and so onwards for the Canaries, and *fell with* Fuerte-ventura," etc.—Sir W. Ralegh.

67 As the ships were close in with Java or Madura on the twentieth, it seems probable that the shoals here obscurely described are those which lie northward of Kangelang Island.

68 *Ruinata.* There is no island now so called; but in a chart said to be "examined with the most expert cardes of the Portingales pilots," A.D. 1598, appears *Ranata*—an island of considerable size. Its bearing and distance from the south-western extremity of Celebes lead me to consider it as Zalinaf and the group of isles which lie north of it. If so, the shoal-water was on the Laar Bank.—Linschoten; J. Horsburgh.

69 *And so bearing up.* The impropriety of this phrase has bee admitted. It is the *helm* which is *borne up;* the *ship*, in consequence, *bears away*—or runs before the wind.—W. Falconer.

Smith and Thomas Dawson. The twenty-eighth day we fell with Celebes, being high land, and at four a-clock in the evening we came to an anchor in twenty-six fathoms, sandy ground, four leagues from land. The twenty-ninth in the morning we weighed, steering east along the land; and the general went in our pinnace alongst the land to seek for fresh water, for that he greatly doubted it was the Bantam water[70] that killed our men, but he lost his labour, and returned without any, for there was none to be found: at night we anchored in thirty fathoms water; this morning died William Paret of the flux. The thirtieth day we passed the Straits of Celebes,[71] and shaped our course for the Isles of Bouton. The thirty-first in the morning we were fair by the land of Bouton, and all the night lay by the lee.[72]

The first of February we held on our course with a fair wind;[73] the second died of the flux Henry Lambert; the third day died of the flux Edward Smith; the fourth in the morning we had sight of Amblaw and Bouro, being two islands; this day died Henry James, the fifth day Richard Miller died of the flux. The sixth day we were fair by the land Amblaw, and our general went in the pinnace to seek for fresh water, and went with the people of the country, and they brought him to a fine sandy bay, where there was

70 The Bantam water should have been avoided: it must have been too impure for use. The Dutch made this unwelcome discovery soon after their first arrival there: "Les Hollandais qui s'amusoient à en boire s'en trouvèrent très-mal, et perdirent même des gens par les maladies qu'elle leur causa."—C. de Renneville.

71 By the Straits of Celebes we are to understand what is now called Salayer Strait. This appears by the chart of the *Moluques* by Jean C. de Moye, circa A.D. 1614.—C. de Renneville.

72 To *lie by the lee*, an obsolete phrase, is the same as *lie-to*. It is performed, under shortened canvass, by keeping one sail full, while another is laid aback. The ship, therefore, makes no head-way.—W. Falconer.

73 It seems the ships ran to the eastward of Bouton, for when captain David Middleton passed through the narrow strait to the westward of it, on his return from the Malucos in 1608, the raja declared that he had never seen any Englishmen.—Purchas.

very good water; and there they took in three baricos,[74] and brought aboard, and would spend no longer time there because it was towards night, and Amboina so near at hand.

The seventh day we had sight of Amboina, and of a ship which played off and on the land, but would not come and speak with us. This afternoon we were fair by Amboina, and the wind very variable, but it fell calm, so that we could not get in.[75] The eighth day at ten a-clock came up a gale of wind, which brought us to Amboina shore, where we coasted with our ship very near, but could not have any ground to anchor in, for that all the islands have very deep water hard aboard the shore;[76] we came to a bay, where we found sixty fathoms water, and there we anchored, and the Indians brought us some fruits to sell. This afternoon we saw two Hollanders' pinnaces under the shore of Veranula,[77] which came out from under the land to show themselves to us, but did return back. The people of Veranula be great enemies to the Portugals, and had sent to Bantam to the Hollanders, desiring their aid to expel the Portugals out of these islands; which if they performed, they would become subject to them, and sell none of their cloves to any other nation but them. This I knew to be true, for that the parties who were sent to

74 *Baricos.* From the Spanish *barrica*=a small barrel. The word was in common use: "The cooper is to looke to the caske, hoopes and twigs, to staue or repaire the buckets, *baricos*, cans," etc.—Capt. Smith.

75 The author must mean *get in with the land*—not *get into* the Bay of Amboina. They were certainly on the north shore of the island, and steering towards its north-eastern extremity.

76 *Aboard the shore.* A curious nautical phrase, which I shall explain by an example: "I myself coasted in my barge close *aboard the shore*, and landed in every cove, the better to know the island [Trinidad], while the ships kept the channel."—Sir W. Ralegh.

77 In accordance with the text, Veranula would seem to be some part of the opposite shore of Ceram. Master Scott, however, leads us to infer that it was some part of Amboina. Argensola, on the other hand, describes it as a large island adjacent to Amboina; with a city of the same name, which was plundered and burnt by André Furtado de Mendoça in 1602. I cannot solve this problem.—E. Scott; L. de Argensola.

Bantam, I have often spoken withal.[78] This day died of the flux our master his mate, Thomas Michell. The ninth day we watered, but could not come to the speech[79] of any of the country people: this afternoon died Thomas Eldred of the flux. The tenth day we weighed anchor, and stood to the eastern end of Amboina, and came to an anchor in an hundred fathoms water, fair by the shore, fair by a town called Mamalla.[80] Before we came to an anchor there came an Indian aboard of us which spake good Portuguese; also there came a letter to our general from the captain of Amboina,[81] but it was directed to the general of the Hollanders, or any other captain of his fleet, supposing us to be Hollanders. The effect of his letter was, to desire them to certify them of some news of Portingal, and to send an answer by any of his people of his letter, who should be very welcome, and should both safely come and go. The general went this day a-land, and delivered a present to one they called their king, and other great men, and did desire to know whether we might have trade or no; they made answer, that they could not trade with us without license of the fort. This night died of the flux Mark Taylor.

The eleventh day our general sent a letter, by John Rogers, to the captain of the fort, and divers of the principal of the town of Mamalla accompanied him thither to have license to

78 Three youths, sons of three chiefs, arrived at Bantam from Amboina on the fifteenth of July 1604, to solicit aid against "certaine Portingales which had a smalle forte there, and did sore anoy them." They were often entertained at our factory.—E. Scott.

79 *Come to the speech.* An admissible phrase, witness a masterly writer before quoted: "We abode there [Punto de Gallo] four or five days, and in all that time we *came not to the speech* of any Indian or Spaniard."—Sir W. Ralegh.

80 Mamalla, or Mamalà as we have it in Argensola, lies towards the north-east extremity of the island. It appears in the *Plan of the Island of Amboina*, published by Dalrymple in 1782.

81 The commander at Amboina was Gaspar de Melo, who soon afterwards lost his command and his life.—Manoel de Faria y Sousa.

trade with us, which they had granted them by the captain. The effect of our general's letter was to certify him of the death of our queen, and peace between England and Spain,[82] with other news of Christendom; and for better confirmation of truth, he sent the captain of the fort our king's majesty and the prince's pictures, with divers of his majesty's new coin; and in conclusion, as there was peace with our princes and their subjects in Christendom, he desired that the like might be between us, for that our coming was to seek trade with them and the Amboinians, which he hoped he would not deny him.[83] The party which carried our general's letter was very kindly entertained by the captain and soldiers, but that night permitted not him to come within the fort, but lay in a good lodging without the walls, where he was visited by the principal of them. This evening five sail of Hollanders[84] were entered into the mouth of the harbour, and turning up for the fort.

The twelfth, the forenamed Hollanders came to an anchor within musket shot of the fort,[85] the Portugals not offering to shoot at them. This afternoon John Rogers returned with an answer of the letter, and there came in his company a

82 The treaty of peace between James I. and Philip III. was concluded at London on the eighteenth of August 1604. The news was carried to Bantam by admiral van der Hagen.—*Articles of peace;* E. Scott.

83 The general was recommended to touch at Amboina, or at any island on the way where cloves might be had, in order that he might the less depend on the result of his mercantile proceedings at Banda—the place of his destination.—*Instructions*, § 26.

84 *The Dutch fleet.* The Dutch fleet sailed from Bantam on the seventeeth of January 1605, N.S. It consisted of "nine tall ships, besides pinnaces and sloops", viz.: *Les Provinces-unies*, 700 tons, admiral van der Hagen; the *Dordrecht*, 700 tons, vice-admiral Sebastiaanz; the *Amsterdam*, 700 tons; the *Hoorn*, 700 tons; the *Gueldres*, 500 tons; etc. A yacht and two sloops had been sent to cruise soon after their departure from Bantam: the remainder of this formidable fleet seems to have arrived in company at Amboina.—E. Scott; C. de Renneville.

85 The fort is on the south-east side of the Bay, and not much less than twenty miles from Mamalla. It was afterwards called Fort Victoria.

Portugal soldier, which brought a warrant from the captain to the governor of Mamalla[86] to trade with us, and likewise to give John Rogers for his pains a bahar[87] of cloves, which was presently delivered him.

Before the coming away of John Rogers, the Portugals, with a flag of truce, went aboard the Dutch admiral to know wherefore they came thither; if in friendship, they should be welcome—if otherwise, to give them a direct answer.[88] The Dutch general made answer that his coming thither was to have that castle from them, and willed them to deliver him the keys, and they should be kindly dealt withal; which, if they refused to do, he willed them to provide for themselves to defend it, for that he was minded to have it before he departed, and that his staying was but for the rest of his fleet, which as then were in sight—therefore willed them by fair means to yield. The Portugals made answer, the castle was their king's, and of sufficient strength, and therefore willed them to depart thence; and as he came as a messenger, in way of truce, they desired they might have free liberty to depart, which was granted them, with an

[86] The former edition has *Manillia*, and so it stands in two other instances. It should be Mamalla, as before. See note 80.

[87] *Bahar*—a Malay word, from the Arabic. It is a weight equal to about 560lb.—but varying in different places.—W. Marsden.

[88] The importance of Amboina as a colonial possession, and the defects of the above narrative of its capture, induce me to give the Dutch account of that event entire:—

The Dutch fleet. "Le 21 [de Février 1605, N.S.] sur le soir, la flotte mouilla l'ancre dans la baie d'Amboine, du côté du nord. Le lendemain, on mit à terre des gens qui marchèrent droit vers le fort des Portugais. Mais avant qu'ils eussent pris poste, le gouverneur du fort envoya deux Portugais dans un canot, avec une lettre, à bord de l'amiral. Cette lettre était pour demander ce que la flotte venait chercher en ce lieu, et ce qu'on prétendait faire contre un fort qui lui avait été confié par le roi d'Espagne. L'amiral fit réponse, sur-le-champ, qu'il était venu là par ordre du prince Maurice, pour se rendre maître du fort d'Amboine. Cette réponse ayant beaucoup alarmé les deux Portugais, ils prirent congé, et promirent de revenir dire quelle résolution le gouverneur aurait prise."

answer in writing to the captain, willing him to surrender up this fort unto him, in the prince of Orange his name, by two a-clock that day, or look for the extremity of war; what after passed betwixt them I know not. The answer of our general's letter from the captain of the fort was, that he and all the Portugals in the place were exceeding glad of the good news we brought them of that long and wished for peace between our nations, and that there was not anything in their power in that island wherein they might pleasure us but we should command it; and as touching the cloves of Mamalla, he had sent special order to the governor to make sale of all they might make at a reasonable price; and likewise he had good store of cloves in his castle, which should be all ours, if pleased the general to come with what speed he could thither, whereby he hoped to come to some good composition with the Hollanders. This day died of the flux, Daniel Aske. The thirteenth we weighed our anchors to come ride nearer the shore of Mamalla; but our general made the Portingal soldier believe he weighed to go to the fort, which was no part of his meaning, for that there was not any hope of good to be done for us, the Hollanders being there before us; but before we came to an anchor we heard

Cependant les vaisseaux s'étant approchés du fort, autant qu'il fut possible, laissèrent tomber l'ancre sur les dix heures du matin, et le canonèrent. Le gouverneur voyant les forces des Hollandais, et la manière dont ils l'attaquaient, n'osa s'exposer à l'assaut qu'on lui préparait, et offrit de capituler.

Après plusieurs conférences entre ses députés et l'amiral, il fut conclu, que tous les Portugais point mariés se retiréraient; qu'il serait libre à ceux qui étaient mariés, de demeurer, en prêtant le serment de fidélité au nom des Etats Généraux et du prince Maurice; que chacun pourrait emporter un fusil, ou un mousquet, et que tout le canon, toutes les munitions, et les armes du roi, demeuréraient dans le fort.

En exécution de la capitulation, l'amiral se rendit au fort avec cinquante hommes, et y fit arborer un étendard. Les vaisseaux célébrèrent cette conquête par des décharges d'artillerie et de mousqueterie. La place était fort bien pourvue de canon, et d'autres munitions. Il y avait environ trente pièces de fonte. Le nombre des Portugais qui furent

ordnance go off, so that we made account the fight was begun between them, for that the Portingal soldier told our general they would never yield up their fort, but fight it out to the last man, with many other brags of their strength and resolution, which afterwards proved to be nothing but words. This day our general went a-land with some merchandise to barter with them, but nothing was done that day, but put off till the next day.

The fourteenth our merchants went ashore with commodities, and the chief of the town came and priced our wares, which they liked very well, but offered very little for them; and for such cloves as they had they would not sell under one hundred reals-of-eight[89] the bahar, which made show they had no will to deal with us. The Portingal soldier went a-land with our general, with a letter to his captain, and four yards of green cloth, given him for a reward; but when they came to talk with the people to know what news at the fort, some said it was taken, others said they were in fight, but in these doubts there came a messenger from the fort, which brought us certain news it was yielded to the Hollanders by composition, but upon what conditions I knew not. The Portingal soldier hearing this certain news durst not return, for fear the people would cut his throat by

chassés du fort et de l'île, était de près de six cents, à qui les Hollandais donnèrent deux vaisseaux qu'ils avaient auparavant pris, et les envoyèrent. Il demeura encore dans l'île quarante six familles Portugaises, qui prêtèrent le serment de fidélité.

Cette victoire fut considérable, non-seulement parce qu'elle coûta peu, n'ayant point coûté de sang, mais parce que cette place et cette île étaient d'une grande importance.—C. de Renneville.

This bloodless conquest was attended by one tragic circumstance. Gaspar de Melo, the governor of the fort, was apprehensive of being disgraced, and his wife, to save his honour, took away his life by poison!—Manoel de Faria y Sousa.

89 *Reals-of-eight*—a semi-translation of the Spanish term *reales de á ocho*. Reals-of-eight, of the same value as the Spanish, were coined at our mint for the convenience of the East-India company; also halves, quarters, and half-quarters.—Rogers Ruding.

the way, but desired the general he might tarry with him, which he granted;[90] and after the governor of the town had heard that the Hollanders had the castle, he then told our general he would sell us no cloves without licence of the Hollanders, so that all hope of trade in this place was gone. The fifteenth day we took in water and made partition of the merchandise to the Ascension, for she had taken none in at Bantam, but all was put into our ship, by reason they were so exceeding weak they were not able to stow them.

Here our general was almost in despair for the attaining of his lading, and especially for cloves, nutmegs, and mace. We heard they had good store at Banda, but the Hollanders were there before us with great store of such commodities as we had, which they had taken in a ship bound to the Malucos, laden with the same commodities; yet there was hope of the Banda commodities, which is nuts and mace, by reason of the great quantity we heard say they had: likewise this day the general called a council of the captains, masters, and merchants,[91] and there told them that there was no way left us to attain to our lading but to part company, and the Ascension to go for the isles of Banda to seek her lading of nutmegs and mace; and that he was minded, with the Dragon, to go to the Malucos, or else at leastwise to do his best to get thither.[92]

[90] This anecdote seems to prove that the Portuguese had made themselves hateful to the natives, and it is certain that Manoel de Faria condemns the conduct of his countrymen in very pointed terms.—Manoel de Faria y Sousa.

[91] This was a special council—not provided for in the instructions. The advice of the masters was of more importance on such an occasion than that of the merchants.—*Instructions*, § 2.

[92] In three previous instances the term *Malucos* has been used to comprise all the *spice* islands, as Amboina, Banda, etc. See note 60. It is here used, with more propriety, to denote the *clove* islands which lie west of Gilolo. The credit of attempting to reach those islands is entirely due to captain Henry Middleton. It was more than those who framed the instructions ventured to propose.—*Instructions*, § 26.

This speech of his was disliked of all, for that in both our ships at that present were not so many serviceable men as would sail the Ascension, and therefore we should hazard both the ships to part company, having so weak a company; and likewise to attempt the voyage to the Malucos, it was against reason, for that we had both the wind and current against us,[93] and to ply it to windward with so weak a company it would be lost labour. This was the opinion of all, saving the general, who still had a good hope we should attain it. At this time nothing was concluded, but left to be considered upon till the next morning.

The sixteenth day, very early in the morning, before day, master Grove[94] came to the general's bed-side, telling him he could take no rest all the night for thinking of the motion made by him and our going to the Malucos: although it was a thing never attempted by any, yet he saw no other way [than] to put it in practice, otherwise we must make account to return back to Bantam without lading.

The general was glad to hear him of that mind, and at the coming aboard of captain Colthurst and his master, it was absolutely determined upon to part company, although greatly to the dislike of them both, for they thought never to see us again, our weakness in both ships being so exceeding weak: the seventeenth day we weighed and plied to windward all the day and all the night, to get to sea the way we came in. The eighteenth day we got to sea clear of Amboina, and

[93] The author alludes to the monsoons, or periodical winds which prevail in the Java, Banda, Maluco and other seas. In the Maluco passage, what is elsewhere called the south-east monsoon blows nearly south from April to October, and what is called the north-west monsoon blows nearly north from November till the end of March. Now the course from the Bouro Strait to the Maluco islands is due north: they had therefore to contend with an adverse wind and surface-current.—D'Aprés de Mannevillette; J. Horsburgh.

[94] Master Grove was master of the Dragon, as the circumstances abovestated prove. When named in a subsequent paragraph, he is called *Grave*. It may be an error of the press.

stood to sea till the afternoon, and then we parted company with the Ascension, [she] bearing up for Banda afore the wind, not having passing a day-and-a-half sail.[95]

From the eighteenth to the one-and-twentieth we plied it and got very little to windward; this day it fell calm, and we were carried between two islands—they be called Manipa and *Ambovzeylioe*—[96] with a great current, and lost more in the calm in one night than we had got in two days. The general sent his brother to Manipa to buy fresh victuals; but everything was so dear, they came without, saving a couple of goats the king sent our general for a present.

The king of this isle used our men very kindly and feasted them, being very glad to hear of the health of our queen. He asked for sir Francis Drake: this king was at Ternatè when sir Francis Drake was there.[97] The two-and-twentieth day we anchored under Manipa, on the south-west side, in fifty fathoms: this day died Thomas Harman, of the flux. The three-and-twentieth we weighed with very much ado, for our anchor was foul of a rock; we broke one of the flooks thereof before we could weigh it. The twenty-fourth day most part calm, in which calms we were carried very near

[95] *The Ascension.* "The twentieth day of February the Ascension arrived at Banda, and anchored in four-fathoms-and-a-half by Nera, which is the chiefest place in those islands. From the south part of Amboina to Banda, the course is east-by-south, to the *southward* thirty leagues [sic]. The latitude of Banda is four degrees forty minutes [4° 31′ S. Horsburgh.], and the going-in is to the westward. There is a very high hill that burneth continually, and that hill you must leave on the larboard side, and the other great island on your starboard side. The going-in is very narrow, and you cannot see it till you come within half-a-mile, but fear not to stand with the island that the high hill is on, [*Gunong-api*] while you come within two cables' length of it, for so you must do, and then you shall have about twenty fathoms; and then stand along still by that island about a cable's length from it, if the wind will give you leave, and then you shall find shallower water, eight, seven, six fathoms, and in the very narrow of all, you shall have five fathoms, and so that depth until you come into the road. By God's help, a man may go in without any danger, keeping near unto the aforenamed island [*Gunong-*

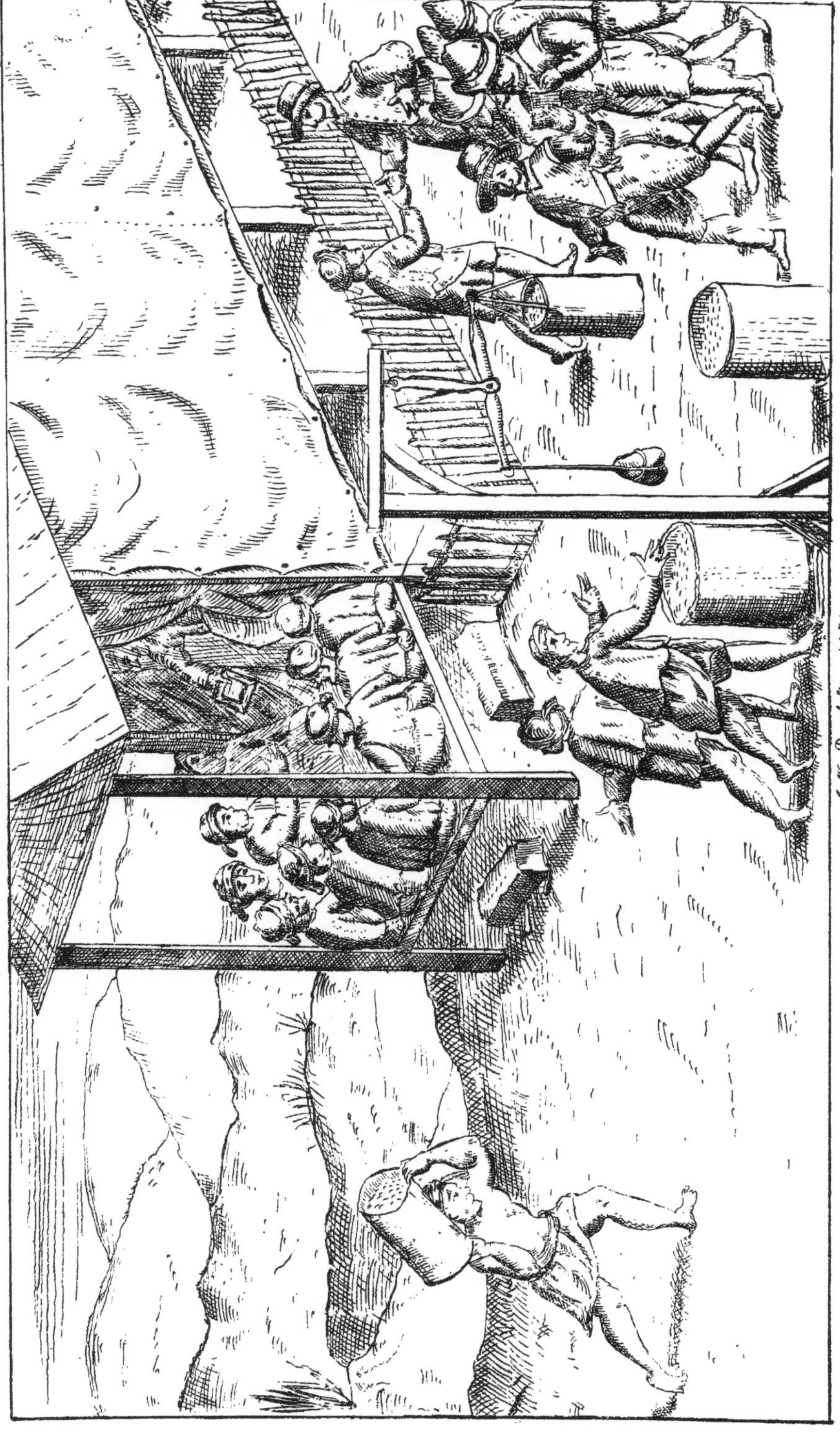

Manipa shore, all sails standing, and upon a sudden came a gust which had like to have put us upon a ledge of rocks which we had no way to avoid but, all sails standing, came to an anchor: we anchored within a quoit's cast of the rocks, and so escaped that danger. The twenty-fifth day died Thomas Beynes. The twenty-seventh day, much rain, the wind westerly.

March the first, the winds all northerly: this day died of the flux, Thomas Wheeler. The second day the wind at the north-west for the most part: this day died of the flux, Richard Hedges and William Flud.

The third day we came fair by an island not specified in our *cards*:[98] it lieth west-south-west from the southernmost island of Bachian, some fourteen leagues. This isle off Bachian, we gave to name *Haul-bowline*, for that in seven days' sailing we got not a mile. The fourth and fifth days we plied all we might, but could do no good, and those few sound men we had were tired with continual labour; we at this present lacking both wood and water, came to an anchor under Haul-bowline in sixty fathoms: [at] this time the master and boatswain were both very sick of the flux, inso-

api]. It is somewhat shallow on the starboard side, in the narrow of the going-in, but that will show itself. There are two small islands, one called *Pulo-way*, and the other *Pulo-rin*, and they lie about three leagues to the westward of the going-in. There is no danger about them but may be very well perceived. You may leave those islands on which side you please, either at your going in, or coming out."—T. Clayborne.

[96] Manipa, in the Bouro Strait, has preserved its euphonic name. For *Ambovzeylioe*, I am inclined to read *Amblaw-island*.

[97] Sir Francis Drake reached Ternatè, in the course of his famous circumnavigation, in 1579. He was received with much pomp and courtesy. The king was said to be "Lord of an hundred islands."—*The world encompassed.*

[98] *Cards.* Johnson imperfectly defines the word *card.* I shall prove its signification by his own example:

"Upon his *cards* and compass firms his eye,
The masters of his long experiment." *Spenser.*

Now, the cards and compass were distinct articles. The *cards* were *charts.*

much that the general was in great doubt of their recovery. The sixth day very much wind at north-west; our general went a-land to seek for fresh water, but could find none, but digging a well in the sand we found very good water; as for wood we needed not to seek for that, the island yielded nothing but wood to the sea-side, that one was scarce able to pass, the trees and brakes were so thick: here our Portingal soldier was very sick of the flux, and the general was very careful of him, for that he hoped by his means to have trade with the Portingals of Tidorè for cloves. The seventh, eighth, and ninth days, we spent in wooding and watering, which we got all aboard. The ninth day the winds continuing northerly, with much rain: this day died of the flux, William Elmesmore. The tenth day we weighed, but had much ado to get up a small anchor; our weakness was so great that we could not start it without tackles: this day died David Flud. The eleventh day rainy weather, the wind at north-west we stood to the north-east-ward: this day died one of our merchants, called master George Ware, of the flux. The twelfth, thirteenth, and fourteenth days we spent in turning to windward, sometimes upon one tack, sometimes of the other: the thirteenth day died Edward Ambrose, of the flux. The fifteenth and sixteenth days, the winds easterly, we made some nineteen leagues north-west.[99]

The seventeenth day we were in ten minutes of south

[99] The conclusion of the *extract* which follows is somewhat in advance of the text, but as it chiefly relates to the monsoons, and does not admit of division, it is inserted here:

The Ascension—at Banda. "About the middle of March here, we found the wind to be variable, and so continued till the middle of April; and then it continued and stood between the east and south-east, four months to our knowledge. But it doth use to continue five months, as the people of the country say, and likewise five months between the west and north-west, and the other two months variable. Here in the dark moons it is given much to gusty weather, and much rain. Here we staid one-and-twenty weeks and six days, in the which time we had eleven men died, and most of the flux."—T. Clayborne.

latitude, the winds all westerly, and we ran some ten leagues north: this day we had sight of all the clove islands,[100] that is to say, Maquian, Motir, Tidorè, and Ternatè, all of them picked hills in form of a sugar-loaf. The eighteenth and nineteenth days we were fair under the land of Maquian, between that and Gilolo, where the people of Maquian came aboard of us with fresh victuals, but sold very dear. They said they had good store of cloves in the island, but they could not sell us any without leave of the king of Ternatè. The twentieth and twenty-first we spent plying to windward, with little wind, between Maquian and Motir: this island of Motir is uninhabited, but hath great store of cloves upon it. This island standeth between Tidorè and Maquian, but nearer to Maquian by one-third of the way than it is to Tidorè: the people of this island have been slain most part in the wars between Ternatè and Tidorè—for sometime it was subject to one king, and sometime to another.

The twenty-second day we got under the land of Tidorè, and bearing up between a small island called *Pulo Cavallie*[101] and Tidorè, there came rowing two of their galleys from Ternatè, making all the speed possible they could toward us; the headmost of the two waving with a white flag unto us to strike sail, and to tarry for them. At the same time came seven Tidorè galleys, rowing betwixt us and the shore, to chase the Ternatan galleys—we not knowing their pretence.

100 We now witness, with regard to captain Henry Middleton, the achievement of that object which was the principal motive to early maritime enterprise. As Fletcher, the dramatist, says—

"We are arriv'd among the blessed islands
Where every wind that rises blows perfumes,
And every breath of air is like an incense."—*Island princess*, I. 3.

Five islands are enumerated by most geographers, viz. Ternatè, Tidorè, Motir, Maquian, and Bachian. The writer omits the latter. The *Bachian* of Schouten and others, I take to be the *Benchan* of Derfelden van Hinderstein. A copy of part of his chart accompanies this volume.

101 *Pulo Cavallie*, in the chart published by Horsburgh, is called *Pot-bakers-island. Pulo*, a Malay word, means island.—W. Marsden.

They in the Ternatè galleys did all they might to overtake our ship, waving with two or three flags at once to tarry for them, which our general seeing, caused the top-sails to be struck, and lay by the lee to know what was the matter ; so that the foremost of these galleys or caracoas[102] recovered our ship, wherein was the king of Ternatè, and divers of his noblemen, and three Dutch merchants.[103] When they had fast hold of the ship, the Dutch merchants showed themselves to us, looking pale, and desired our general for God's sake to rescue the caracoa that came after us, wherein were divers Dutchmen which were like to fall into the enemies' hands, where there was no hope of mercy, but present death—whereupon our general caused our gunner to shoot at the Tidorè galleys, yet that would not cause them to leave their chase, but within shot of our ordnance discharged all their shot at the Ternatè galley, and presently boarded them, and put all to the sword, saving three men which saved their lives by swimming, and were taken up by our men in our boat: there were no Dutchmen in her as they reported, but all Ternatans. If we had not tarried as we did, the king of Ternatè, and those with him, had fallen into his enemies' hand, where no hope of mercy was to be expected. The Dutch merchants coming aboard, told our general they thought we had been Hollanders, and bound for Ternatè, and that was the cause they had put themselves in such danger, and likewise to know whither we were bound: our general told him that he was going then for Tidorè, to seek trade with the Portugals, with whom we were in amity. They dissuaded the general not to attempt any such thing,

102 *Caracoa.* A rowing boat used in the eastern seas. The word occurs near twenty times, and is variously spelt. I have given it the Spanish form. The Malay term is *kōra-kōra.*—W. Marsden.

103 The Dutch fleet had not yet arrived from Amboina, and the *merchants* who had so narrow an escape must therefore have been some of those who were left in charge of the factory which had been established here on a former occasion.—C. de Renneville.

for there was no other thing to be expected at their hands but treachery: the general answered he knew them well enough, but minded to work so warily with them, that he doubted not of any harm they could do him.

The Dutchmen seeing our general minded to go to the Portugal town of Tidorè, desired him that he would not let the king of Ternatè and them fall into their enemies' hand, whom so lately he had delivered them from ; and as for cloves, there was good store to be had at Ternatè and Maquian, and for their parts, they would not be our hindrance, for that they had neither wares nor money left. So the general caused them to entreat the king to come into the ship, who came in trembling, which the general seeing, thought he was a-cold, and caused his man to fetch him a black damask gown, laid with gold lace, and lined with unshorn velvet, which the king put upon his back, but never had the manners to surrender it again, but kept it as his own. The king being in the general's cabin, desired him to go with him to Ternatè, where he minded to have a factory; but himself and his ship would make no stay there, but go to Tidorè, to see what usage he should find of the Portugals.

The king did what he could to persuade him to the contrary, but could not prevail.[104] Here the general delivered a letter from the king's majesty of England,[105] with a fair standing cup, and a cover double-gilt, with divers of the choicest *pintados*, which he kindly accepted of, and presently had the letter read, and interpreted unto him, wherewith he made show to be greatly contented.

104 The early history of the Maluco islands is that of a perpetual contest between the kings of Ternatè and Tidorè. Hence their mutual jealousies and criminations. It was just so when sir Francis Drake visited the islands twenty-five years before this date.—L. de Argensola ; *The world encompassed.*

105 This royal letter is printed in the *Appendix*. *Pintados*, adopted from the Spanish word *pintado*=painted, denote the coloured scarves wherewith the natives "gird their loins."—E. Scott.

We trimmed our sails by a wind, and plied to windward for Ternatè; the king's caracoa not daring to put from the ship. About four of the clock in the afternoon came the king of Ternatè's eldest son aboard in a light frigate,[106] which rowed well: he greatly doubted the welfare of his father, and the king stood in doubt of his son. At his coming to his father aboard our ship, in the general's cabin, he kissed his father's right foot, and he kissed his head. The general had given warning to all his company, that they should tell no news of the Hollands fleet, but before night it was told the king and all the rest, but by whom could never be learned. From the twenty-second to the twenty-fourth, the king and all his crew tarried aboard of us. The four-and-twentieth day we came by the chief town of Ternatè,[107] and saluted them with seven pieces of ordnance; the same afternoon we came to an anchor in the road, which is in the *southest* [south-east] part of the island, in fourteen fathoms, sandy ground: the road is from the town two leagues and a half. The twenty-fifth day the king sent for his plate and victuals from the town, and feasted the general in his own cabin. There sat none of his nobles with him at table; none sat but his son and the general: the rest sat upon the floor of the cabin cross-legged, like tailors. After dinner the general desired him that he would take some order he might have a house to establish a factory, for that he was minded to go to the Portugals to see what he could do with them. The king persuaded him earnestly not to meddle with them, for he was sure there was nothing but villany and treachery with

[106] *A light frigate.* The term *frigate* was not in use till the sixteenth century. It meant a small open vessel, furnished with oars and sails. Le seigneur de Villamont says, "Entrans donc en la *fregate,* nous remontasmes en nostre *naue.*"—A. Jal; S. de Villamont.

[107] The chief town of Ternatè, at that date, was Gammèlammè. It was near the south-west extremity of the island. A view of the town as it appeared in 1599, when admiral van Warwyck established the Dutch factory, is added to this edition of the voyage.—C. de Renneville.

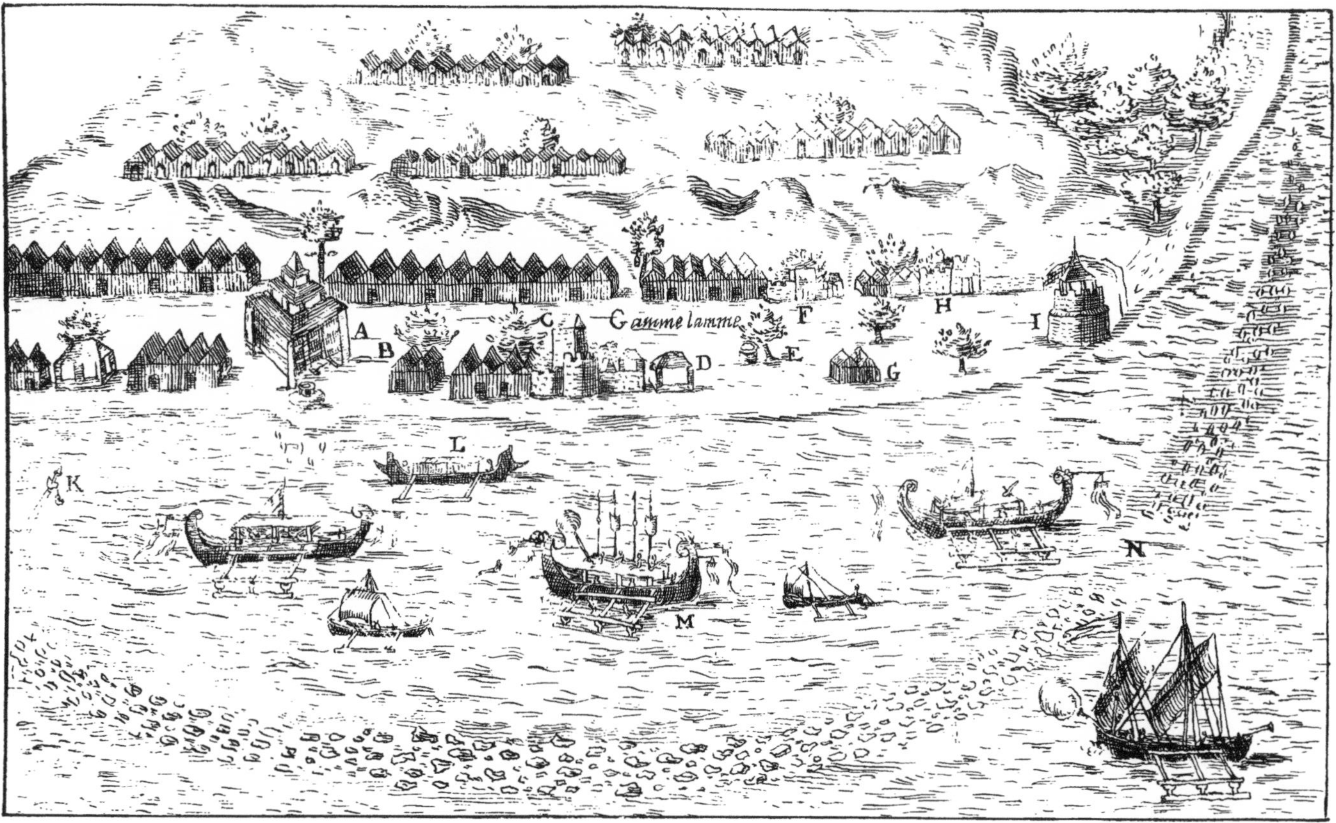
Gamme lamme
A
B
C
D
E
F
G
H
I
K
L
M
N

them. The general said it was a folly to dissuade him from it, and therefore prayed him that he might have a house according to his promise. The king, seeing in what earnestness the general did speak unto him, said he would presently depart to the town, and cause a house to be provided in a readiness for his merchants.

The twenty-sixth, before day, our general was in a readiness, with such merchants and merchandises as he minded to leave at Ternatè, [and] went to the town, and an hour before day came thither. The king, hearing a noise of trumpets, knew that our general was come, and sent a small prāu to our pinnace to will our general to come unto him. He was aboard the admiral of the caracoas. He came into our pinnace, and sat some half-an-hour there taking tobacco, and then came the sabandar[108] with light, and brought the general to his house, and the king to his caracoa. Our general, presently after his landing, caused his men to land all our goods, and carry them to the house, which was performed before daylight. Then the Dutch merchants invited the general and master Brown[109] to dine with them, with whom they presently went to the Dutch house, where they showed them what every sort of commodities were worth in that place, with proffers of any kindness they could do him. As for the prices of our wares the general had made inquiry of the Guzerats which came aboard, which did agree with the Dutchmen in rating of every sort of them, whereby he knew that they did not dissemble.

Before it was dinner time, there came a messenger from

[108] *Sabandar.* The former edition has *sabandor,* with remarkable uniformity. *Sabandar,* however, is the customary orthography. *Shabandara,* a Malay word from the Persian, denotes the officer of state who superintends the affairs of the port and customs.—W. Marsden.

[109] Master Brown, one of the principal merchants, and a member of the council, was left at Bantam next in rank to his more famous associate master Gabriel Towerson, and appointed to succeed him in the event of his death.—*Appendix.*

the king to will the Dutch merchants to come and speak with him, and the general came home to our house, where he had not staid half-an-hour, but one of the Dutch merchants came for him to come speak with the king. So the general taking master Brown, and John Addeyes, one that had the language,[110] and myself with him, went presently with them that were present, where we found the king in a large room, sitting in a chair, and all his chief councillors about him sitting upon mats on the ground; before him, the Dutch merchants, sitting among them. When the general came, the king willed him to sit down. After he was *set* [seated], the king caused the letter brought by our general from the king's majesty of England to be openly read—which being done, the king acknowledged himself beholding unto his majesty for so kind a letter, and a present, which he would endeavour to requite; and for confirmation thereof he gave his subjects free leave to trade with us for cloves, and likewise as one wishing us all the good he could, he desired our general for his own good, that he would not have anything to do with his enemies, the king of Tidorè and the Portugals, with whom he should find nothing but treason and treachery.

The general, by his interpreter, gave him great thanks for his kindness in giving so free liberty to trade with his people, and likewise for his good counsel to shun the treachery of the Portugals, but for his part he doubted no treachery at all should harm him, for that he did mind to stand upon such a guard as all the strength they had should not offend him; and therefore desired his highness to pardon him he did not follow his counsel, for that he purposed with all speed to go

[110] It is doubtful whether John Addeyes, or some person not named, is the "one that had the language". Augustine Spalding was the interpreter at Bantam. He went out with captain Lancaster in 1601, remained near twelve years in the eastern islands, and in 1614 dedicated to sir Thomas Smith a small volume entitled *Dialogves in the English and Malaiane languages*, from the Latin of Arthusius—a publication which was suggested by Hakluyt.—E. Scott; *Dialogves*, etc.

thither, and to offer them peaceable trade, which if they refused, he had the thing he desired—then had he just cause to be at war with them, and if they would not accept of peaceable trade, he minded to join with the Hollanders against them, when God should send them thither.

This speech of the general contented the king and all there present, so that they had no more to say, but entreat him that he did not furnish them with any of our great ordnance, and to take great care of their treachery: and so the council broke up, the general taking his leave of the king and all his nobles, for presently after dinner he minded to depart aboard; also the king promised, if the Portingals would not trade with us, he would write his letter to the governor of Maquian to deal with us, for all the cloves in that isle. And so the general and master Brown went to the Dutch house to dinner; which being done, he came home with the Dutch merchants in his company. And so, taking leave of them and of us, departed aboard.

The twenty-seventh day in the morning came aboard two men, sent by the king of Ternatè, with a letter to the governor of Maquian to trade with us. They were sent by the king to go along with us thither, for our better usage. So about eight a-clock in the morning we weighed, and plied it all day for the road of Tidorè; and about sun-setting we came to an anchor, in thirty-two fathoms sandy ground, on the western side of the isle, fair off, by the shore.[111] Coming to an anchor, there came a caracoa with two swift canoes to take view of our ship. Our general commanded one to wave them with a white flag; and presently one of the small prāus came fair by us, demanding whence we were. Our general caused our Portingal soldier to will them to come aboard,

[111] The text may be correct, but there is room for suspicion. The anchorage at Tidorè is "on the *east* side of the island, near the town, in thirty fathoms, sandy bottom." The town so situated bears the same name as the island.—J. Horsburgh.

for we were Englishmen and their friends. And so there came aboard us three Portingals, which entered into the gallery,[112] and went into the general's cabin, where the general told them, his coming thither was to seek trade with them as friends, for that the wars between our nations was done, and a peace concluded—the queen of England being dead, and the king of Scots king of England. They made answer, that they knew that the queen was dead, by way of the Philippines; and to hear of the long-desired peace they were very glad, and for trade with us they said they could say nothing till that they had made the captain acquainted therewith: and because it was night, they were desirous to be gone, promising the next day morning to return. So the general let them depart, and our Portingal soldier with them, with a letter to the captain of the fort, wherein he did certify him of the news of Christendom, and the cause of our coming thither; and so they departed.

The twenty-eighth day, about six a-clock, we weighed, having very little wind, and at eight aclock came a caracoa, and two prāus from the Portingals' town, and in them five Portingals, and our above-named soldier. The general stood in the waist,[113] and entertained them; our soldier telling the general, the principal of them was called Thomè de Torres,[114] captain of a galeon, and the rest married men of the town. Captain de Torres delivered our general a letter from the captain of the fort; the effect was, that he was welcome with all his company to him and all the rest of the Portingals

[112] *The gallery.* The principal entering-ladder of a ship was made of wood, and placed amidships. The *gallery-ladder* was made of rope, and chiefly used in foul weather.—Capt. Smith.

[113] *The waist.* Why the visitors were not received on the quarter-deck is unexplained. The *waist* was "that part of the ship betwixt the main-mast and the forecastle."—Capt. Smith.

[114] The former edition has *Thome Detoris,* and in other instances *Torris.* I conceive we should read *de Torres.* Captain de Torres acts a conspicuous part in the narrative of occurrences at Tidorè.

inhabiting in that place; and whereas the king of Ternatè and the Hollanders their enemies had given bad reports of them, saying there was nothing but villany and treason to be had at their hands, he hoped our general did conceive better of them, and that their reports were of malice and not of truth, and no credit to be given to the report of their enemies, but experience should prove them liars, and themselves no such bad-minded people; and therefore he willed the general to have no doubt of good usage at their hands, and for trade which he desired with them, he would resolve him thereof the next day—for as yet they had not called a council concerning that matter, without which council he could not do it, but willed him to have no doubt thereof. So the general took them down to his cabin to breakfast, and the caracoa and the boats towed the ship to the town-wards, being very little wind. About eleven a-clock we came to an anchor, a little to the northwards of the fort, and saluted the fort and town[115] with seven pieces of ordnance, and from the fort [were] answered with three pieces; and presently upon the same, in a boat came the captain of the fort, called Pedro Alvaro de Abreu, and the captain of the other galeon, called Fernando Pereira de Sande:[116] these galeons that these captains did belong to, did ride within a league of rocks, very near the shore, with their broadsides to seaward, with ordnance placed therein to shoot at their enemies, which come rowing by them sundry times. The general brought the captain of the fort and the other captain down with the rest to break-

[115] The town of Tidorè, and the Portuguese fort, were thus described in the journal of Matelief, in 1607: "La ville de Tidore est située sur la côte orientale de cette isle, et est tellement environnée de bois, que lorsqu'on en est seulement à une portée de mousquet, on n'en peut presque pas voir quatre ou cinq maisons.—Le vieux fort des Portugais *est* couvert de broussailles."—C. de Renneville.

[116] The former edition has *Petro Alleneris Debbroo* and *Ferdinando Perrera de Sandy*—for which names I have ventured to substitute those above-printed.

fast, the captain of the fort making great haste to be gone. After many compliments passed between our general and them, they took their leave and departed, promising the next day to come look upon our commodities, and to agree upon price for them. About three a-clock our general sent his brother ashore with presents to the three captains, which they very kindly accepted; the captain of the fort returning the general a fat beef.[117]

The twenty-ninth day came captain de Torres and other Portingals aboard, and the general caused our merchants to bring a note of all such commodities as were in our ship into his cabin, where he showed every sort unto them, setting a price upon them. Captain de Torres and the rest of the Portingals said they were too dear at such rates, saying and protesting they sold better cheap[118] suchlike commodities one to the other, and therefore desired the general to be more reasonable, and then he should have all the cloves in the island. The general withdrew himself apart, and in writing set down his lowest prices, how he would sell, willing them to go a-land and consider of it, and return with an answer, if they could, that night; so they took their leave and went ashore.

The thirtieth day captain de Torres came aboard, and would have abatement of each sort of commodities, which the general would not yield unto; telling him, if he would not give such prices, he would be gone for Maquian, and upon the same presented the two Ternatans which the king sent to him for the same purpose. So he seeing nothing would be abated of that price, agreed with the general, and appointed his own dwelling-house for our factory, with many kind proffers, which he faithfully performed.

[117] This is no vulgarism—but a remarkable instance of the mutability of language. For "returning the *general* a fat *beef*," we should now say "returning the *admiral* a fat *ox*."

[118] *Better cheap*. *Chepe* may be equivalent to *market*—but surely *good cheap* and *better cheap* are gallicisms. They correspond with the phrases—*à bon marché*, *à meilleur marché*.—Nares.

The thirty-first, being Easter day, captain de Torres with divers of the principal men of the town dined aboard with our general.

April the first, in the morning, the general sent his brother and master Woodnoth[119] with merchandise a-land to captain de Torres' house, and within an hour after, the general went a-land himself, where he was visited by the king, the captain of the fort, and all the principal men of the town, who entertained him most kindly. They staid some small time with him, and departed all of them. They being gone, the general began to set his merchants a-work, to buy cloves of the Portingals; and having set them in a ready way how to deal with them, he went with captain de Torres to dinner, where there was no lack of good cheer. After dinner came the high priest to welcome our general, willing him to have no doubt of any bad dealing in that place: upon his soul he would undertake, that there were not any in the town that wished him or any of his company any harm, with many other compliments, and so departed. Captain de Torres made offer to the general to be his chief factor, and to help his brother and master Woodnoth in their business, each having more to do than they could well turn them to: and to say the truth, he was so careful in their business, as if it had been his own. This day died of the flux, master Mitten our cook; and of the flux, Thomas Halls. The Tidoreans came not aboard to sell us any thing; the general doubted it was long of[120] the Portingals, who had put them in some needless fear.

The sixth day the general sent his brother to the king of

[119] Master George Woodnoth, a merchant, was left at Bantam next in rank to master Brown, and was to succeed to the command of the factory if Towerson and Brown should die.—*Appendix*.

[120] *It was long of the Portingals.* *Long of* is synonymous with *owing to*, as in Shakspere: "You, mistress, all this coil is *long of* you." M. N. D., Act 3, sc. 2. I know not why *long* is printed as an abbreviated word by the editors of our dramatist.

Tidorè with a present, and to divers of his principal men, desiring his highness he would give his subjects leave to repair aboard with cloves, and fresh victuals, and that there was no cause of fear why they should abstain from so doing. The king said, they should have leave to bring us refreshing aboard; but for the cloves his people had, [they] should be brought to the English house, otherwise the quantity we should buy would not be known, whereby the king of Portingal might lose his custom; and presently upon the same the king made a proclamation, willing all his people to repair to the English factory with such cloves as they had. The captain of the fort proclaiming the like in his town, there came a flying report the Hollanders were in sight, and upon the same the king sent out a caracoa to sea, but saw no shipping.

The ninth day the general sent his brother ashore again unto the king, with a present, to desire his highness to give his subjects leave to repair aboard with their cloves, for that the Portingals would not permit them to repair to his house, but would be served themselves with the best wares, and let his people have but their leavings. Whereupon the king promised they should come aboard; which they afterwards did.

The twelfth day came news the Hollanders were in sight, and out went the bloody colours[121] at the fort. The fourteenth day, being Sunday, captain de Torres, the king's factor, and divers other of the principal of the Portingals, dined with the general. This day the captain of the fort sent our general

[121] The *bloody colours.* The *white flag* was a sign of amity, or submission; the *red flag*, of defiance. Witness the extract which follows: "Les ennemis [savoir, les Portugais] connaissant bien que nous n'étions pas gens à les abandonner, arborèrent un petit pavillon blanc. Le commis s'en étant aperçu, en avertit le maître, qui fit ôter le pavillon rouge, et cesser de tirer. Mais le pavillon blanc des ennemis fut incontinent ôté; car, ainsi que nous l'apprîmes depuis, il y avaient des contestations entre eux. Enfin—ôtant le pavillon royal, ils y remirent le pavillon blanc, pour marque qu'ils demandaient à parlementer."—C. de Renneville.

word, that the Hollanders were off and on Bachian,[122] willing the general to cause his factors to get in his debts that were owing before their coming.

The fifteenth day the general sent his brother ashore to gather in such debts as were owing, and likewise to buy cloves if any came to the house to be sold, which he performed, buying some small quantity, for that most in the island were in our hands, without it were some eighty bahars which the king's factor had, which he could not sell, because they did belong unto the merchants of Malacca.[123] The captain of the fort gave commandment to all men to make present payment, which they honestly performed. The general sent to captain de Torres to know the cause: he sent him word we had bought all they had, without it were those which were in the factor's hands, which could not be sold.

The nineteenth day we prepared for our departure from hence, to go to Maquian. The twentieth day came a Portingal aboard with a letter to our general from the captain of the fort, the effect thereof I could not learn. The king of Ternatè's two men, which all this time of our being in this place had tarried aboard, were very earnest with the general for their departure to the isle of Maquian, where they made no doubt but to lade our ship with cloves. They began to be merry to see us in such readiness to be gone, for they lived in no small fear of some treason to be attempted against us

[122] *Bachian.* I take this to be the *small* island then so called. In the *Rutter* of master John Davis, of Limehouse, it is said to be in 30′ N. Capt. Humfrey Fitz-herbert, describing the large island now called Bachan, says "There is another near adjoining called old Bachan." This seems to decide the question. See note 100.—Purchas.

[123] Malacca was one of the most important cities in possession of the Portuguese, being considered as the key to the China seas and the eastern archipelago. It was unsuccessfully besieged by the Dutch, assisted by the king of Johor, in 1606; and was afterwards the scene of a desperate sea-fight between the Dutch and Portuguese. The loss sustained by the latter was believed to have hastened the death of the viceroy Martin Affonso de Castro.—Manoel de Faria y Sousa; C. de Renneville.

by the Portingals and Tidoreans, in so much that all the time of our being here they were the best watchmen in our ship. The general sent his brother to the king, desiring his highness he would write his letter to the governor of Taffasoa to sell him such cloves as they had there, which he presently did. This town of Taffasoa is upon Maquian and holds for the king of Tidorè ; all the rest of the island is the king's of Ternatè.

The twenty-first day, being Sunday, came the same Portingal that brought our general the letter the day before, with commendations from his captain to the general, and to certify him the Hollanders' ships were in sight. The Portingal taking his leave, about eleven a-clock we weighed with a small favorable gale of wind, to go for Maquian. As we passed by the fort we saluted them with five pieces, they answering us with three. Likewise, coming thwart the king's town we gave them five pieces, and were answered with six from the galeons. At this present we had sight of the Hollanders.[124] Captain de Torres, our general's great friend, coming aboard presented him with hens, which be both scarce and dear, and so took his leave. We keeping on our course with little wind for Maquian, passing between Motir and Pulo Cavallie, the Hollanders seeing us come room[125] upon them, were in good hope we had been a Portingal

[124] *The Dutch fleet.* "Après cette expédition [à Amboine], il fut arrêté que cinq vaisseaux, savoir le Vice-amiral [le Dordrecht], Ouest-Frise, Amsterdam, Gueldres, et Medenblick, iraient à Tidor ; que l'amiral prendrait la route de Banda ; et que le Hoorn demeurerait à Amboine pour y prendre sa charge. La chose ayant été exécutée, ces cinq premiers vaisseaux se rendirent le 1 de Mai 1605 [N. S.] sur la côte de l'isle Poulo Cavely, où ils apprirent d'un amiral Anglais [Middleton], qu'il avait chargé une petite partie de clou de girofle à Tidor, et qu'il avait dessein d'aller à Macian, pour tâcher d'y prendre le reste de sa cargaison."—C. de Renneville.

[125] To *come room* seems to denote an alteration of the course from *sailing by the wind* to *sailing large*—as in this extract: "And the admiral weathering us, *came room* upon us," etc.—Sir R. Hawkins.

that for fear was flying away. Night being at hand, they spread themselves that we could not pass them but one or other must needs see us. About midnight we came amongst them, sounding our trumpets,[126] whereby they did know we were not Portingals. The admiral sent his skipper[127] in his pinnace aboard to know what news, which was certified them at full. He departing, they saluted us with three pieces of ordnance: we answered them with the like. They told our general that they had taken Amboina castle, and left a garrison therein.

The twenty-second day we came to an anchor about seven a-clock at night, a little to the eastward of the chief town of Maquian: the town is called Mofficia, in which town the viceroy for the king of Ternatè is resident. This afternoon came a caracoa aboard before we came to an anchor, and told our general they would go about the isle, and to all the towns, to give them warning to repair to our ship with their cloves before night. They had compassed the island, and came aboard us again.

The twenty-third day the general sent his brother, with the two Ternatans and the king's letters, and a present to the governor. The present he received, and caused the letter to be publicly read; but for the cloves of that island, he said they were not ripe, but those few that were to be had, the general should have them the next day. This day died of the flux, our baker Griffith Powell.

The twenty-fourth day the general went ashore himself to the governor, to know why the people came not with cloves according to promise. He made answer, he thought

[126] *Trumpets.* There was always a trumpeter in an armed ship. His station was, the poop. He sounded on occasions of ceremony; in time of action; and as a mode of hailing. We meet with the phrases, *hail with whistles, hail with trumpets.*—Capt. Smith; etc.

[127] *Skipper.* The former edition has *shiper.* It is the Dutch word *schipper.* The skipper of a merchant vessel was the commander. In an armed ship, his duties were those of the master.—W. Welwod.

there were not any ripe in the island, but he had sent to all the towns to warn them to bring in cloves; which they would not fail on the morrow.[128] The general seeing their delays, began to suspect the king of Ternatè's letter was to command them to sell us none: therefore, if they came not the next day, he would go to Taffasoa. Much quarrel and war is between those of this place and they of the island; and if there be any taken of either part, the most favour they show them is to cut off their heads.

The twenty-fifth day came most of the chief men of the island aboard to our general, and told him they had small store of ripe cloves in the island, which they were willing he should have. But they were sent for by the king of Ternatè, to repair with their forces to assist him in his wars against the king of Tidorè and the Portingals; and therefore desired him not to be offended with them, for that they could not sell him cloves till the wars were done. This day they of Taffasoa had taken ten men of this town, and cut off their heads.

The twenty-sixth we weighed, with very little wind, and plied it for Taffasoa, which standeth on the west-north-west part of the island.

The twenty-seventh day the general sent his brother in his pinnace to the town of Taffasoa with the king of Tidorè's letter, which he delivered. The governor having read it made answer, that all the cloves they could make the general should have; for that the king had sent him word in another letter, which he received the day before, that he should cause

[128] We have seen that Bantam was the principal mart for pepper, and that Banda was noted for producing the best nutmegs. We now see that cloves were the coveted article at the Maluco Islands. On another valuable article, also produced there, the writer is silent—it is *sago*. Pigafetta describes it in his account of the circumnavigation attempted by Magalhaens; and sir Francis Drake, when he touched at those islands in 1579, made of it "the greatest quantity of his provision."—Pigafetta; *The world encompassed.*

all in the town to be sold him. The Portingals have a small block-house[129] with three pieces of ordnance in this town, wherein were five Portingals: they had some cloves which they promised the general should have. The pinnace returned, and brought one of the Portingals aboard, the ship lying becalmed all the time of their absence.

The twenty-eighth day, about ten a-clock in the morning, we came to an anchor right before the town of Taffasoa, in seventy fathom water, hard by the shore.[130]

The twenty-ninth day the general went a-land to the governor, who offered himself and town to be at his disposition, saying his king commanded him so to do. The general demanded whether the people would bring their cloves aboard: he made answer they had small store of boats, and could not therefore so conveniently come aboard. So the general told him he would set up a tent upon the strand, right against the ship, if he would cause his people to bring them thither. He liked well thereof, and came down with the general to choose out a convenient place, and so took his leave; promising, so soon as the general sent aboard, to will them to make provision to set up a tent—which in two hours after was done.

The thirtieth day was an alarum in the town, their enemies having taken a man without the walls, and cut off his head. The king of Tidorè hath soldiers there, which keep good watch and ward; the town standing upon a point of a land, close by the sea, and is compassed with a wall. The king of Ternatè hath twice attempted with all his force to take it, but could do no good. They live in such fear, they

129 *Block-house.* This compound word, omitted by the early glossarists, occurs in Lambard, Stow, and Carew. The latter says, "Foy hauen—receyueth this name of the riuer, and bestoweth the same on the town. His entrance is garded with *block houses.*"—R. Carew.

130 *Taffasoa.* On Taffasoa, the scene of a sharp contest, see p. 46. The town is noticed ten times in the course of the narrative, and spelt uniformly. Elsewhere it is spelt *Taffasor.*

dare not at any time go a flight-shot out of their walls without a guard of soldiers. They have often truce, but they break it upon slight occasions. A little before night the governor came to our general, and told him there were no more cloves to be had, and therefore he presently caused the tent to be pulled down, and sent all things aboard.

The second day [of May], in the morning, our general received a letter from the captain of the fort, wherein he certified him of the burning of the two galeons by the Hollanders, and entreated him to make speed thither to see the fight which he daily expected, and to bring those five Portingals with him which were at Taffasoa; willing the general, that he should come to an anchor before the king's town, where he should have all the cloves they had.

The third day, in the afternoon, we came before the king's town, where we found all the Hollanders riding, and let fall an anchor amongst them, in a hundred fathoms, fair by the shore. The king of Ternatè was likewise there, with all his caracoas. After the mooring of our ship the general sent master Grove,[131] our master, to the Dutch admiral, who found but cold entertainment; the Dutch affirming we had assisted the Portingals in the last fight,[132] whereby they had received great hurt, and that they were told so by a Guzerat. The master denied it, and said the Guzerat lied like a dog; saying, if the general had done so, he would not deny it for any

[131] The former edition has *Grave*. See note 94. I shall assume that Grove was a Fleming, and the person who was afterwards master of the Ascension, which was lost on a shoal, some twenty leagues from Surat, on the fifth of September 1609. She was then under the command of captain Alexander Sharpey. The crew escaped in two small boats, and arrived safe at Gundavee.—Purchas; Robert Coverte.

[132] I cannot repel this charge. The author of the *Conqvista de las Islas Malvcas* says Middleton furnished the Portuguese with six barrels of powder, a hundred cannon-balls, and a number of morions. His words are, "Diole seis barriles de poluora, cien valas de artilleria, y buen numero de morriones. Con esto se començaron los Tydores y Portugueses à fortificar."—Bart. Leonardo de Argensola.

fear of them, but justify it to their faces, either here or anywhere else. These hot speeches being overpassed they grew into milder terms, and then they began to tell our master the manner of their fight with the galeons, and the burning of them, with the loss of some of their men in the same fight;[133] and they minded the next day to fall down to the fort and lay battery to it—which they had done before, if the king of Ternatè had not withheld them, in persuading them to tarry for more help, which he expected from the other islands. So the master having learned what news he could, came aboard and told the general what speeches had passed. An hour after the master's coming aboard, there came a prāu from the king's town with a letter to our general from captain de Torres, wherein there was nothing but commendations, and that he would come aboard when it was dark and see him. The general willed him to come; either night or day he should be welcome. This evening the king of Ternatè rowed over for Batochina [Gilolo] with all his caracoas; and captain de Torres came aboard to see our general, tarrying some two hours, telling the general they desired to fight with the Hollanders, not doubting of victory; and for such cloves as they had, they should be brought to the king's town, and so conveyed aboard us. So growing very late he took his leave and departed ashore.

[133] *The Dutch fleet.* "Le 2 de Mai 1605 [N.S.] les cinq vaisseaux mouillèrent l'ancre à Tidor, devant le palais du roi, pour parler à ce prince. Pendant qu'ils étaient là mouillés, ils découvrirent deux caraques qui étaient tout-à-terre, entre deux retranchements qui pouvaient fort bien les défendre.

Le 5 le vice-amiral ayant fait sommer le fort de Tidor, ceux qui le gardaient répondirent qu'ils se défendraient jusqu'à la dernière extrémité. Avant que de l'attaquer, les Hollandais jugèrent à propos de tâcher de se rendre maîtres des deux caraques, et le vice-amiral s'avança de ce côté-là, accompagné du Gueldres, dont le capitaine se nommait Jean Jansz Mol, homme de mérite et de beaucoup de courage.

Ces deux vaisseaux s'étant approchés des caraques commencèrent à leur envoyer leurs bordées, à quoi les Portugais, tant ceux qui étaient aux retranchements, que ceux qui étaient dans les vaisseaux, répondirent assez

The fifth day the Hollanders expected the coming of the king of Ternatè, but he came not.

The sixth day our general sent his brother and master Woodnoth to the king of Tidorè, to know if he would sell them any cloves. He made answer, at that time all his people were busy in fortifying the town, so that he could not spare them from their work, but bade the general assure himself of all the cloves that he and the Portingals had. This night came one of our men in a small caracoa from Ternatè, and told our general that they were hardly used by the king of Ternatè in not suffering them to buy and sell with his people, according to promise, and had taken their weight from them, giving commandment that no man should sell them any cloves. Likewise he said that they could get no victuals for their money, because of the wars, and that all our men were very sick, save master Brown. The king, by his caracoa, sent the Hollanders word he would be with them in the morning.

The seventh day, in the morning, came the king of Ternatè with all his forces, and he himself went aboard the Hollands admiral, where most part of the forenoon was spent in council; and about one of the clock the ships weighed, and came under their foretopsails fair by the fort, and let fly all their ordnance, the fort shooting now and then a piece at them. They came to an anchor a little to the northwards of the fort, where they spent the most part of that

bien de leur grosse artillerie et des mousquets ; de sorte qu'il semblait que c'était une grêle de boulets et de balles. Un trompette qui était sur la hune d'un autre vaisseau en fut abattu, et tomba sur le pont.

Pendant qu'on tirait ainsi de part et d'autre, le vice-amiral et le capitaine Mol firent armer leurs deux chaloupes, qui nonobstant la grêle qui tombait, abordèrent les caraques, et les prirent, après un combat d'une heure. La plus grande partie des gens des équipages s'était jetée à la mer pour se sauver, ayant auparavant mis des mèches ardentes et des étoupins aux poudres, pour faire sauter leurs caraques ; de quoi, par bonheur, les Hollandais s'aperçurent en y entrant.

Ces derniers perdirent trois hommes en ce combat, et ils en eurent

afternoon in shooting at it, but harmed them not at all. The Portingals could not harm the ships as they rode, having but one piece laid out that way. In the hottest of this battery,[134] the king of Ternatè and the Hollanders landed some of their forces a little to the northward of the town: not finding any resistance, they intrenched themselves where they landed, in the sand, and there continued all the night without molestation. After the Hollanders had done their battery, captain de Torres came aboard to see our general, where he was very merry and pleasant; saying, as always he had, that they nothing doubted of a happy victory—and for such ordnance as had been shot at them, it had done them no harm at all, only he was sorry that the ordnance did hinder them for bringing of cloves to him. But he desired the general to have a little patience, and he should not want cloves to lade his ship; which were nothing but words, for it was well known to the general he had but eighty bahars in the town, which the factor had.

The eighth day, very early in the morning, the ships began to batter the fort, which continued the most part of the morning; in which time those men of the Hollanders which lodged a-land had brought themselves within saker-shot of the fort,[135] and there raised a mount, whereon they placed a great piece of ordnance and began their battery, the Portingals now and then shooting a piece to no purpose.

The ninth day, before it was light, the ships began their

dix-sept de blessés. Ils enlevèrent des caraques sept pièces de canon de fonte, savoir trois grosses et deux petites; puis ils y mirent le feu, et les laissèrent voguer à la merci des vagues."—C. de Renneville.

134 *Battery.* The word *battery*, at this period, was almost always used to denote the action of battering—not the platform where ordnance was mounted.—*English expositor.*

135 *Within saker-shot of the fort.* A saker was a piece of ordnance of three-and-a-half inches bore. Its extreme range was estimated at seventeen hundred paces.—Capt. Smith.

battery, and they likewise from the mount,[136] and upon a sudden the Dutch and the Ternatans sallied out of their trenches with scaling ladders, and had entered upon the walls before the Portingals in the fort were aware, and had placed their colours upon their ramparts; which the Portingals seeing, came with a charge upon them, with shot and fire-works, throwing at them which were so mounted, that they cast down their weapons and leaped down far faster than they came up, leaving their colours and their furniture behind them—the Portingals still continuing throwing of fire-works amongst them, whereby divers were hurt and scalded. At such time as the Hollanders gave the scalado, thirty of the choicest Portingals, with great number of the Tidoreans, were going in the woods to give an assault upon the backs of them which were lodged where the piece of ordnance was mounted; in which time of their absence the Hollanders entered upon their walls. If these men had been in the fort it had gone far worse with the Hollanders. The

[136] *The Dutch fleet.* "Le 14 de Mai [N.S.] cent cinquante Hollandais descendirent à terre, sous le commandement du capitaine Mol, qui était assisté d'un capitaine Zélandois nommé de la Perre. Ils marchèrent vers deux villages, l'un situé au sud, l'autre au nord, qui appartenaient aux Portugais, et les brûlèrent. Le roi de Ternate, qui était là venu, avec quatorze caracores ou vaisseaux, montés chacun de cent quarante hommes d'équipage, en mena cinq cents à terre avec lui pour être spectateurs du combat, et en même temps pour tenir le roi de Tidor en respect, afin qu'il ne secourût pas les Portugais.

Cependant la flotte s'étant avancée au nord du fort avait commencé à le canonner, et à la faveur du feu qu'elle faisait le capitaine Mol avec ses cent cinquante hommes faisait ses approches. Il fit faire un retranchement de tonneaux remplis de terre, et y fit travailler avec tant d'ardeur qu'il fut très promptement achevé. Ensuite il fit tirer sur la place, et ceux qui la gardaient ne s'épargnèrent pas non plus à tirer sur lui.

Comme les matelots ne sont pas propres à faire longtems la guerre sur terre, le capitaine Mol crut qu'il devait se hâter. Il prit deux soldats avec lui, et étant allé de nuit visiter secrètement la place de tous les côtés, il vit qu'il y avait déja une brèche raisonnable; de sorte qu'il fit préparer ses gens pour livrer assaut le lendemain.

Ce jour-là, qui était le 19 de Mai 1605, les deux capitaines menèrent

Portingals that were abroad, hearing the alarum at the fort, came running back again, and some that ran fastest came to the walls at such time as they in the fort had put them to the retreat, where they went to handy-blows with them. Captain de Torres, which had the leading of the thirty men, was shot with a musket and slain. By this time the most of the thirty Portingals were gotten some within and some under the walls ; and the Hollanders and Ternatans throwing away their weapons, began to take their heels to run into the sea. At this very instant, when the Portingals and the Tidoreans had the victory in their hands, and very ready to charge upon their flying enemies, the fort took fire and blew up even with the ground ; so that all the Portingals which were under the walls of the fort were there buried, and the most part within the fort were blown up into the air. The captain being newly gone out to place two soldiers at a little postern door, gave them charge to kill any Portingals which should go out that way,

dès le matin leurs gens jusqu'au pied du fort, et cela se fit si secrètement que les ennemis ne s'en apperçurent pas. D'un autre côté les vaisseaux ne cessèrent pas de faire jouer le canon, jusqu'à ce que Mol fût prêt à donner l'assaut, ce qu'il fit connaître par le moyen d'un étendard qu'il fit élever, auquel signal ils ne tirèrent plus.

Alors ce vaillant capitaine allant à la brèche, à la tête de ses gens, et ayant une enseigne à la main, entra dans la place avec sept hommes, après un long et opiniâtre combat. Les Portugais qui s'étaient retirés dans la tour firent un si grand feu sur ceux qui entraient dans le fort, et leur jetèrent tant de balles d'artifices, dont l'enseigne même que tenait le capitaine fut toute brûlée, que personne n'osait plus s'y hasarder. Enfin ils reprirent si bien courage, et se défendirent si vigoureusement, que le capitaine et les sept hommes qui l'avaient suivi furent aussi obligés de se retirer.

En sortant par la brèche le capitaine tomba, et se cassa une jambe. Quelques-uns de ses gens ayant couru à lui pour le prendre et l'emporter, il ne voulut pas permettre, et les exhorta vivement à retourner à l'assaut. Mais comme on admirait son courage, et qu'on voulait le sauver presque malgré lui, un homme robuste s'approcha, le mit sur ses épaules, et l'emporta.

Dans ce premier assaut, un capitaine d'une des caraques qui avaient

in which time of his absence the fort was blown up, whereby his life was saved; but how, or by what means it took fire, it could not be known. The Hollanders and Ternatans seeing the fort blown up, began to gather up their scattered weapons, and made a stand, not daring to enter the ruins of the fort till the Portingals had left it; which was half-an-hour after. In which time the Portingal and Tidorean slaves had sacked the town, setting fire on the factory where the cloves were, which they could not carry with them, leaving nothing of any worth behind them. When the king of Ternatè saw the victory on his side, he with all the caracoas came rowing towards the king's town in triumph; but durst not come very near, for that the king of Tidorè did shoot at them. And so rowing by our ship, singing and making great mirth, returned to the fort, where was no resistance; but so long as the Portingals had it he durst not come within a mile. When the Ternatans had pillaged the town, they set all the houses a-fire, which were quickly burnt even with the ground, being all made of canes. After

été brûlées fut le premier à qui Mol eut affaire. Il vint, armé de toutes pièces, attaquer le Hollandais, l'épée à la main, et prétendait le percer. Mais Mol ayant détourné le coup avec sa demi-pique, un de ses mousquetaires qui s'était avancé tira sur le Portugais et lui cassa la tête.

Les Hollandais ne s'étant pas rebutés de cette première disgrâce, retournèrent à l'assaut, où ils furent repoussés plus facilement cette seconde fois qu'ils ne l'avaient été la première. Ces avantages relevèrent tellement le courage des Portugais qu'ils chassèrent leurs ennemis jusqu'à la moitié du chemin de leurs retranchements.

Ceux qui étaient sur les vaisseaux, voyant ce qui se passait, recommencèrent à canonner le fort. Un boulet tiré du Gueldres contre la tour, tomba sur la poudre, et fit sauter la tour en l'air, avec soixante ou soixante-dix hommes ; accident terrible, et dont la vue faisait frémir. Aussitôt les soldats retournèrent à l'assaut pour la troisième fois, et étant entrés dans le fort, les armes à la main, les Portugais perdirent courage, et demandèrent quartier ; ce qui leur fut accordé.

Dès que cela fut fait, les gens du roi de Ternate, qui n'avaient été que spectateurs, accoururent pour piller, et pour détruire tout ce qu'ils purent jusque-là qu'ils mirent le feu dans une tour de pierre où il y avait beaucoup de clous de girofle. Les Hollandais firent tous leurs efforts

this victory, the king of Tidorè sent his son and a nobleman to our general, desiring him to be a means of peace between the Hollanders and him; for now he had what he desired, which was victory over the Portingals. The general sent him word he would do his best, as well for him as for the Portingals which by fortune of war were fallen into their enemies' hands. So presently the general caused the pinnace to be manned, and he and the master went aboard the Dutch admiral. When they came thither they asked for the admiral, who was ashore; but they sent for him. At his coming he bade our general welcome; after many speeches passed of their fight, and commendations undeserved given of themselves, they exclaimed upon the Ternatans for cowards, and attributed all the glory to themselves, saying they durst not stand by them in the fight, but ran away. After a great deal of vainglorious commendations of themselves, the general was desirous to see what prisoners they had taken of the Portingals: one was brought forth, being one of captain Pereira's soldiers. The general bade him declare a truth in a matter he would ask him: he made answer, if he could he would. Then he asked him what great ordnance, powder, shot, and guns they had from him to assist them: he

pour empêcher ce désordre et cette perte; mais il ne leur fut possible d'arrêter cette brutalité.

Cette nouvelle conquête ne coûta que deux hommes au vainqueurs, et il y en eut sept de blessés, outre le capitaine Mol. Les Portugais perdirent soixante-treize hommes, et en eurent douze de blessés. La plupart des femmes et des enfants s'étaient retirés dans une forte maison, sur une haute montagne qui n'était pas loin du fort, où l'on ne pouvait monter que par un sentier bien étroit, de sorte que le lieu étant presque inaccessible, on ne le pouvait prendre que par la famine, et par le défaut d'eau. Mais quand on leur eut offert des bâtiments pour se retirer, ils s'embarquèrent les uns et les autres au nombre de cinq cents personnes, et prirent la route des Philippines.

Par cette dernière victoire les Portugais furent chassés de toutes les Moluques, sans y posséder plus rien qu'un petit fort dans l'isle Solor, proche de Timor, lequel n'était pas grande chose. Mais elle avait été bien plus difficile à obtenir que celle d'Amboine; et peut-être que sans

answered, he knew not of any; so, turning to the Dutch admiral, he marvelled he should give credit to such untruths reported by a slave. He answered again, such things were told, but he did not believe them to be true. So the general asked what he meant to do with the Portingals his prisoners: he said he would hang them. The general entreated him to show them mercy, considering they did nothing but what all good subjects are bound to do in defence of their king and country; and therefore desired not to take their lives, nor deliver them to the king of Ternatè. He promised, at his entreaty, not any one of them should die nor be delivered to the king of Ternatè; but that he would ship them away to Manilla. The general gave him thanks, taking leave of them, and came rowing along the shore by the king's town, where he took in the captain of the fort and brought him along with him aboard, where he both supped and lodged, and from him had the truth of all the fight, far differing from that which the Hollanders reported. The general told him his going to the Dutch admiral was principally to entreat him to show mercy unto the Portingals; which he promised to perform. The captain gave him great thanks for the care he had of them, saying now all their hope rested upon him; and upon the same he presented the general with a small ruby set in a ring, praying him to wear it for his sake—which the general would not take, saying what he could do for them was in christian charity, and not for reward.

The tenth day, in the morning, our general went aboard the Hollands admiral, to see if he could bring the king of Ternatè and the king of Tidorè and the Hollanders to a

l'accident du feu qui prit aux poudres il aurait fallu abandonner l'entreprise. Quelques-uns crurent que cet embrasement n'avait pas été causé par un boulet de canon, et que ç'avait été un effet de la négligence, ou de l'imprudence des Portugais. Quoi qu'il en soit, sans cet accident, il y a toute apparence que les Hollandais ne seraient pas demeurés victorieux."—C. de Renneville.

peace. The Dutch admiral made answer, the king of Ternatè would be very hardly drawn to any peace with the king of Tidorè, but he, for his part, would be willing thereunto; and if it pleased the king of Tidorè to repair aboard his ship, he should safely come and go to have conference with him. The general thought he could persuade him to come aboard his own ship, so that he would leave two Dutch captains ashore in pledge for him. But to come aboard his ship he was sure he would not. So the Dutch admiral sent two of his chief merchants with the general, to be left as pledges if the king would come aboard; whereupon our general went to the king of Tidorè, and told him what he had done in his behalf, persuading him to come aboard our ship, which he was loath to yield to. The general, seeing him fearful, told him there was no such cause, for that he had brought two Dutch captains to remain as pledges, and that he would leave his brother with them. Then the king was willing, and caused his own boat to be fitted, and embarked himself. Being ready to put off, came the king's sister, and his son weeping as if he had gone to death, [and] detained him in this manner half-an-hour.[137] In the end he put off, but when he was halfway between the shore and the ship, he saw a caracoa rowing off from the fort; which he stood in fear of and would proceed no further, but returned back, promising the next day to come aboard if we would ride with our ship nearer his town.

The eleventh day, in the morning, we weighed, and anchored again before the king's town. The general with his pledges going ashore, there was an alarum in the town, which was suddenly done: the cause was, that a great num-

[137] After a picture of the miseries of war—the destruction of the galeons, the blowing up of the fort, and the death of captain de Torres, in the midst of his confidence of success—it is refreshing to catch a glimpse of the kindly feelings of human nature as shown by the sister and son of the raja of Tidorè. The journalist should have given more anecdotes of the social life of the natives.

ber of the Ternatans had consorted to go rob some outhouses in the king's town, and finding nothing therein set them a-fire. The Tidoreans gave a sudden assault upon them, and had the cutting-off of a dozen of their heads; all the rest hardly escaped by running away. The heads they presented to the king, our general standing by him telling him the cause. The king seemed to be offended with the Hollanders, which had promised that no hostility of war should be offered in this time of parley. The Hollands captains which were in our pinnace seeing the heads, were in no small fear of their own. After the rumour was appeased, the king embarked himself with our general and the captain of the fort.[138] The Dutch merchants and captain Middleton rowed ashore for pledges, but the king and our general came aboard our ship, where they stayed the coming of the Dutch admiral; who coming aboard, was brought down to the king in the general's cabin, and they saluted one the other very friendly. After some little pause, the king said, whereas at your first coming hither you sent me word your coming was not to harm me nor any of my subjects, but to expel the Portingals your enemies out of the land, and make the place open for trade for all nations, and therefore you desired I should not take with them against you; which I performed till such time I did see my mortal enemy the king of Ternatè join with you, so that I was enforced to arm myself against him, who I know desireth nothing so much as the overthow and subversion of my estate, and therefore you have just cause not to blame me for arming myself and people against the invasion of my mortal enemy. And now seeing you have the upper hand of your enemies the Portingals, it resteth in your power to dispose of them

[138] *The captain of the fort.* Pedro Alvaro de Abreu, whose fortunate escape has been described in the preceding paragraph. As we have no further mention of captain Pereira de Sande, it is doubtful whether he survived the conflict.

as you shall think good. Now you have your desire of them, I would know whether you will have peace, or join with the king of Ternatè against me. The Dutch admiral answered, his coming was only to expel the Portingals, which he thanked God was now in his power. And for peace, he said it was the thing he desired with all princes in those parts, and that he would do what in him did lie to make an agreement between the king of Ternatè and him. The king answered, that he desired a good peace, but it could hardly be, for that any slight occasion was daily cause of breach between them.[139] Therefore he desired the Hollanders they would take part with neither, and he doubted not he should have as good as he brought. The admiral answered, he would do what he could to make an agreement; which if he could not bring to pass, he promised the king—taking our general to witness—that he would take part with neither of them. Which speeches greatly contented the king, who excusing himself of not being well, took leave and went ashore. After the king was gone, came the captain of the fort, looking very heavily, as he had just cause; which the Dutch admiral seeing, took him by the hand, bade him be of good cheer, telling him that it was the chance of war, and that the fury being now gone, he minded to deal friendly with him and all the Portingals; willing him to repair aboard, where he should be welcome, and safely go and come. The captain gave him thanks for his kindness. So dinner being ready, and the pledges come from the shore, they dined all with our general, and departed every man to his home.

The twelfth day, being Sunday, the Portingal captain, with six of the principal of them, came aboard to dine with our general, entreatimg him to go with them to the Dutch

[139] The raja of Tidorè was quite aware of the feelings of his subjects; and the intervention of a moderator, at such a moment of excitement, gave no hope of success. It is much the same now as it was in those times.

admiral, and be a means to hasten their departure, which he did; and at his entreaty they were sent away in three pinnaces and a frigate to Manilla, for which they gave the general great thanks. The twelfth day, the general sent his pinnace to Ternatè with provision of victuals to our men which were there; and they returned the next day, and brought our general word of the death of his servant John Abell, for whom he was very sorry.

This thirteenth day our general and the master went to the king of Ternatè, to know whether he would let him leave a factory in his island of Ternatè. He answered, he should, but willed him to return the next day, for that he would call a council concerning the matter, and then would give them an answer. From thence the general went aboard the Dutch admiral, and there told him how the king of Ternatè had promised he should have a factory there—yet nevertheless, if he would buy such wares as we had left, and make payment at Bantam, he should have them. Who answered, he thought the king of Ternatè would not forget himself so much as to grant us a factory, considering he had written to his excellency,[140] and likewise promised him, that they would trade with no nation but with them. And as touching our commodities, he would not deal withal, for that they had two ships which were sent, one to Bengal, and the other to Cambay, to buy such commodities, which they daily expected. Our general said, he had no reason to cross him for leaving a factory there, for that sir Francis Drake had trade in Ternatè before the names of the Hollanders were known in those parts of the world. So for that time

[140] *His excellency.* By his *excellency* we are to understand prince Maurice of Nassau. In the advertisement to the *Recueil des voiages* so often quoted, we read: "La nation Hollandaise—soutenue par la prudence et encouragée par la valeur de son fameux général et gouverneur le prince Maurice de Nassau, est allée heureusement chercher sous un autre ciel, et parmi des peuples barbares, les secours qui lui étaient refusés par ses propres voisins."—C. de Renneville.

they parted, either part to take their best advantage for their adventurers.[141]

The fourteenth day the general went again to the king, to know his answer concerning his factory. He found him aboard a caracoa, and one of the Dutch captains in his company. The general told him his coming was according to his appointment. The king made present answer, he could grant him no factory, for that he had made promise by writing and word to the Hollanders, that no nation should have trade with him or his people, but only they. The general demanded why he had not told him so when he saved him from the Tidoreans; and then he could have told what to have done. He said, both he and his subjects were willing we should tarry there; but the Hollanders did still urge his promise. The general, seeing he could not leave a factory, desired him to send such order to Ternatè that he might have leave to carry those small quantity of cloves as his factors had bought and paid for aboard, and he would trouble neither him nor the Hollanders. The king answered, that within seven days he would be there himself, desiring the general to ride still. He made answer, he lived at too great charges to lie still and do nothing, and therefore could stay no longer, but would be gone the next morning; and so departed from him.

The nineteenth day the general went a-land, and took his leave of the king of Tidorè and all his noblemen, and all the Portingals,[142] they being all sorry for his departure.

The twentieth day we weighed in the morning for Ter-

141 *Adventurers.* The subscribers towards the equipment of a merchant-ship, or fleet of merchant-ships, were so called. The most noted mercantile association at this period was, *The company of merchants adventurers.*—Lewes Roberts.

142 It is said that about four hundred persons of all sorts were shipped for Manilla. A storm overtook them; but, according to the same authority, they arrived safe "by virtue of certain reliques thrown into the water by a Jesuit!"—Manoel de Faria y Sousa.

natè, and at five a-clock in the evening came to an anchor again on the north-east side of Tidorè. This day died of the flux Thomas Richmond.

The twenty-first day, at four of the clock in the morning, we weighed, and about ten a-clock came to an anchor in Ternatè road in sixteen fathoms, fair by one of the Dutch ships, which two days before us came from Tidorè. This ship was to take in her lading of cloves here. This afternoon, the general sent his pinnace to know if the king had sent word to the sabandar to see the delivery of such cloves as was there of ours. The pinnace brought word master Brown was very sick, and all the company which were with him. This afternoon came aboard to our general the king's uncle of Ternatè, called *kechil* Gegogoe.[143] To this man our general told how unkindly he had been used by the king and the Hollanders, and how the king would neither give him leave to buy cloves while he tarried here, nor permit him to leave a factory there, contrary to the promise he made him when he saved both him and the Hollands factors from enemies' hands, which good turn both the one and the other have quite forgotten ; likewise he said he thought the king had been as our kings in christendom are, which never will promise anything but they will perform it. Kechil Gegogoe hearing this, said he would that night go to the king, and then would tell him how much he did dishonour himself to be so overruled by the Hollanders ; and therefore willed the general not to have doubt of leaving a factory, and likewise to trade so long as they tarried here in the despite of the Hollanders. And upon the same, seeming to be angry, he departed, promising the next day to return again. This man could speak Portuguese, whereby the general let

[143] *Kechil* Gegogoe. Kechil, a Malay word, is a title of honour applied to the relatives of the Maluco princes. It is sometimes spelt *cachil*, and has been supposed to be derived from the Arabic.—W. Marsden ; Bart. Leonardo de Argensola.

him understand his mind to the full.[144] He knew sir Francis Drake when he was at Ternatè, and had been aboard his ship with him.

The twenty-second day the general sent his brother again to the town, to know if the sabandar were come from the king with order to deliver the cloves. Captain Middleton found him now come to town, and brought him to our general, who told him he had order to deliver the cloves, and likewise that he should have free liberty to buy and sell as well as the Hollanders; and that the king desired the general not to depart till he came, which should be shortly after the messenger. All this friendship kechil Gegogoe procured. The sabandar and his two sons supped and lodged in the general's cabin that night.

The twenty-sixth [day], being Sunday, kechil Gegogoe was all afternoon with the general in his cabin, where he feasted him in the best manner he could, and gave him a very fair caliver set with bone,[145] and many other things.

The twenty-eighth day the pinnace went to the town to fetch such cloves away as the merchants should buy. The general or his brother still going or coming in her, at this time it was captain Middleton's chance to be in her; and as he and the merchants were busy buying and weighing of cloves, in came a Ternatan, and told them that there was a man that was indebted unto us, that had brought a canoe laden with cloves to pay his debts, and the Hollanders had both carried him and the cloves to their house, because the man was likewise indebted unto them. Out ran our men with weapons, but she was gone before they came, or else if they had not made the more haste, they had not carried

[144] It appears by the above remark that Middleton spoke the Portuguese language, and as Grove spoke the Dutch, and another the Malay, the Red Dragon was well manned as to linguists.

[145] A *caliver*, or *pièce de gros calibre*, was a species of fire-arm invented by the duc de Guise. It was short, but of considerable bore. The stock was sometimes much ornamented.—Capt. Barwick.

them away so easily as they did. The mariners were hired by one of those factors, whose head the general so lately had saved, for a royal-of-eight a man, to do this brave exploit. At their coming aboard they told the general how the Holland factors used them, which he took very evil.

The twenty-ninth day the general went to the town with twenty armed men[146]—some, shot, and some, pikes and halberds—and at his coming, he sent word to the Dutch house they should restore the cloves they had taken away. They told our general that the party had been in their debt these two years, and they could not get him to any payment, and that the king had made proclamation that no man that was indebted unto the Hollanders should sell him any cloves; yet nevertheless they would not be their own judges, but would stand to the judgment of the king, when he should come, and the cloves to remain in the sabandar's hands till the matter was tried. So the general was pacified, threatening to give the bastinado to the factor which was the cause: but after that time, he durst not pass by our doors. This breach betwixt us and the Hollanders caused the king to make the more haste, for that he doubted we would go by the ears with them; and having very few men in the town, he doubted the worst, for that the Hollanders are not beloved of the country people: the cause is, their manifold disorder in their drunkenness[147] against men, but principally against the women.

The first of June, about one of the clock at night, came a caracoa from Tidorè, rowing by our ship, calling to the

[146] The former edition has "20. armed men, some shot, and some pikes, and halberts." The punctuation is vicious. The author means that some of the men bore fire-arms, and the rest, pikes or halberds.—R. Barret.

[147] *Drunkenness.* Dr. Borde, a shrewd observer, gave this character of the Hollanders in 1542—

"And I am a Holander, good cloth I doo make;
To moch of English beare, diuers times I do take."

At Bantam, some three-score years later, complaints were also made by

watch. The general hearing it, knew it was the king that spake, and rose out of his bed, and saluted him by his name: the king did the like to him, and asked him how he knew him in the dark. The general, by his interpreter, said that he knew him by his voice; which caused him to laugh. And so spending some little time in talking, he willed our general to meet him at the town in the morning. The general gave him five pieces of ordnance at his departure, which he took very kindly. They delight much to hear ordnance to go off at pleasure, so that they be not at the cost. When it was day, the general went to the town, and had not staid in his house half-an-hour, but the king came, and spent all the forenoon with him. The general was desirous to know of him whether he should leave a factory or no. He answered, he could not tell, for that it was to be determined by a council; which he had not leisure to call as yet, by reason of much business. He said the Hollanders did threaten him to forsake his country, and to establish a factory at Tidorè, if he did let the English tarry in the country and establish a factory. They saying we were thieves and robbers, and so, if he did trust us, he should find us; saying that Holland was able to set out twenty ships for England's one, and that the king of Holland was stronger by sea than all christendom besides; with many untruths of their own people and country's commendations, and the disparagement of our people and country and of all other christian princes. If this frothy nation may have the trade of the Indians to themselves, which is the thing they hope for, their pride and insolence will be intolerable. The general answered, what Hollander soever he were that had told his highness so, he

master Scott of the "disorder of the *baser sort* of them when their drink was in." Nevertheless, I conceive the fault was rather excessive merry-making on particular occasions, to which seamen are apt to yield, than habitual drunkenness, as they preserved their health better than our own men did—among whom, both on shore and afloat, the mortality was quite appalling.—Andrew Borde; E. Scott.

lied like a traitor; and said he would justify it to their faces; and for their country, if the queen's majesty of England had not pitied their ruin, in sending her forces to withstand the Spaniards, their country had been overrun, and they marked in the faces for traitors and slaves many years ago.[148] And therefore desired the king to inquire of a Spanish renegado which was in the town, and he would certify him of the truth. Then the general demanded whether he should have those cloves which the Flemings had carried away by force. He answered, we should have so many of them as should pay the debt, and the Hollanders should have the rest—which was in the afternoon performed. The king told our general that the morrow he must return for Tidorè, where he must spend three or four days before he could return. In the meantime he gave him leave to buy and sell with his people, and at his return he should have an answer whether he should leave a factory or no. The general entreating him, whilst he tarried in the country, he would let him have a house to lodge in, where he might be near his business and not be forced every night to go aboard. The king promised he should, and so took his leave and departed. An hour after he sent his sabandar to the general, who brought him to a fair chamber, the king sending him a fair gilded bedstead and a Turkey carpet to lie upon;[149] so after that the general was not enforced every night to go aboard, as before time he had done.

The second day, about eight a-clock at night, came a light prāu of Tidorè aboard, with a letter to our general: the effect was, that the king of Tidorè found himself aggrieved with the Hollanders for taking part with the king of Ternatè

[148] This alludes to the assistance given by queen Elizabeth to the states-general of the united provinces of the Netherlands, by a considerable force under Robert earl of Leicester, in the years 1585-7.—Stow.

[149] The Chinese were the principal oversea carriers at this period, but the Turks also traded with Bantam—a circumstance which accounts for the use of such luxuries.—Purchas; E. Scott.

against him; and that upon his sending away of the Portingals they had shot into his town, demanding Taffasoa to be surrendered to procure his peace. The general answered, he thought he needed not fear the Hollanders, for that their shipping would shortly be disposed of to other places, and that at any time for that town, if so it need, he might make his peace. With which answer they returned, making a bold attempt to either come or go, the sea being full of their enemies.

The fifth day the king of Ternatè and the Hollanders' admiral[150] came from Ternatè to conclude of our banishment.

The sixth day the king sent our general word that both he and the Dutch admiral should come face to face before him and his council, to hear what either could say against other. The general sent the king word he had nothing to say against the Dutch, unless he withstood his leaving of a factory there; which, if he did, he desired his highness that they might meet face to face before him to hear what either could say: the king sent word it should be so. The Dutch admiral came to our general's chamber to visit him. Our general asked whether he came to procure his banishment. He answered he was bound to do the best he could for his adventurers. The general told him, the king was minded the next day to know why we should not have a factory in the country as well as they. He said he would challenge the king's own writing and promise.

The seventh day the general waited to be sent for to the

150 *The Dutch-fleet.* The admiral, as he is called, was the vice-admiral Sebastiaanz. I can give no additional account of the part which he acted with regard to Middleton, as the journal of the proceedings of the squadron ends abruptly. The author briefly notices the destruction of the fort at Tidorè, in accordance with the decision of a council of war, and the appointment of certain persons as factors, and mediators between the rival kings. He then records the departure of the Gueldres, commanded by the brave Mol, for Ternatè; whence she sailed to Bantam, and arrived in Holland in May 1606—carrying home the welcome news of their victories over the Portuguese.—C. de Renneville.

king; but seeing nobody came, he sent to know the reason. He sent word he was very busy that day, and could not intend it till the morrow. The Dutch admiral had conference with the king twice this day; where, belike, he had what he desired, for as soon as night came he departed for Tidorè.

The eighth day the king sent his secretary and one of the Dutch merchants unto him, with a letter sealed with hard wax; which seal had two letters, an H and a B, which stood for Hans Beerpot,[151] with a merchant's mark between the letters. This letter they delivered, and told him it was the king's letter to the king of England. The general would not believe the king would send so great a prince as the king of England a letter with so little state, and a merchant's seal upon it. They answered, and if he doubted thereof, they would cause the king to come and justify it. The general said, he would not otherwise believe it. So they left the letter and departed. Half-an-hour after came the king and a great train to our general's chamber—where, saluting him kindly, they sat down upon a trunk together. The king said, I sent you a letter sealed by my secretary, which you have received, making doubt it is not sent by me to so great a king, and delivered with so little state, and sealed with a merchant's seal. Now you heard me say thus much, I hope you are satisfied; the letter is sent by me and none other, therefore prepare yourself to-morrow to be gone.

[151] *Hans Beerpot.* We formerly taxed the Hollanders with having been our teachers as *health-drinkers,* or something worse: they seem to have returned the compliment. In *Hans Beer-Pot,* a comedy printed in 1618, Cornelius Harmants says—

> "Twas strange to see a younker once but drunke
> In Englands kingdome, when I liued there,
> For to be drunke was beggarlike they sayde;
> Now, beggars say they are drunke like gentlemen."

The authorities quoted were Englishmen, but well-acquainted with the Netherlands.—Henry Peacham; D. Belchier.

The general neither would nor durst deliver it to the king of England, willing him to take it again. He would not, but departed.

The ninth, kechil Gegogoe, the king's uncle, hearing how the general had been used by the king and the Hollanders, came to visit him at his chamber, where there passed much talk between them concerning the foresaid counterfeit letter, intended to have been sent, to the disgrace of the general, to the king of England; kechil Gegogoe assuring the general that, if it lay in his power, he would procure of the king that they might leave a factory there.[152] Moreover, that at his next return to him he should know the contents of that base and slanderous letter invented by the Hollanders; and so he departed, with promise to return the next day. The people of the country understanding the Hollanders had procured our banishment, were much offended that the petty prince of Holland, and his, whom they esteemed but debauched drunkards, should be esteemed before the mighty king of England and his subjects; and knowing we were commanded to depart, brought all their commodities to us and none to the Hollanders. Whereat they finding themselves aggrieved, caused our beam that we weighed cloves with to be taken away, but it was restored again by the means of kechil Gegogoe; which the Hollanders perceiving, they sent to their admiral at Tidorè to return to Ternatè; which he did, threatening the king that he would leave him and establish a factory at Tidorè. Whereupon the king, with the unwilling consent of his council, gave order for our banishment; sending the sabandar to our general to will him to linger no longer, but to depart aboard.[153]

[152] We have seen that kechil Gegogoe, our friendly advocate, knew sir Francis Drake; but in *The world encompassed* we read of "*Moro* the kings brother." Now, *Moro* is one of the synonyms of *Gilolo*—and there must have been some misconception.—De Barros; *The world encompassed.*

[153] The departure of the Red Dragon from the Maluco Islands being at hand, it now seems fit to notice the proceedings of the other ships.

The sixteenth day, towards evening, the king of Ternatè with a great company of his nobles came down from the town, landing right against our ship, and caused a tent to be set up—sending for our general to come ashore, which he presently did. The king caused him to sit down by him, excusing himself that we left not a factory there, alleging that the Hollanders enforced him to the contrary; he and his subjects owing them much, which he hoped to pay the next harvest; and that then he would take another order with them: which being done, he caused a letter to be read by his secretary openly, the contents whereof follow at the end of the book. Sealing it up he delivered it to the general, entreating him to return and he should be welcome. Who answered, that it was in vain for the English to return thither so long as the Hollanders bare rule, holding it a disparagement to his nation to give place to them, being so far their inferiors. This communication ended by the sudden coming of a great many of lights, and in the midst one of his chief noblemen under a canopy, carrying, in a platter of gold, covered with a coverture of cloth of gold, the letter which was before so publicly read; and the general looking earnestly, not knowing what the matter was, the king called unto him, willing him to arise and receive the letter he sent to the king of England. Which he presently doing, the party which carried it made low obeisance after their coun-

The Hector and the Susan remained at Bantam, to take in pepper, till the fourth of March. Captain Stiles dying just before that date, captain Keeling succeeded to the command of the Hector, and master Edward Highlord to that of the Susan. The masters of both ships also died there, and many of the principal men and sailors. Guzerats and Chinese were therefore hired to assist in working the ships on the homeward voyage. Their departure is thus described by Scott :—" The fourth of March the Hector and Susan set sail for England ; the Hector having sixty-three persons in her of all sorts, English and others—but many of her own men being sick. The Susan, so near as I could learn, had forty-seven of all sorts—also many Englishmen sick. *I pray God send us good news of her*." We shall hear more of the Hector and Susan at

try fashion, and then delivered it to the general; which he kissing received, and sat him down again by the king, giving him thanks in doing our king and himself that right in delivering the letter in such sort as it ought to be. The king answered: this letter which you have is unsealed, and written in the Malay tongue, to the intent at Bantam it might be interpreted by some of your own people which have learned that language; but the other was invented by the Hollanders to have done you injury—telling him in brief the effect thereof, excusing himself that he had no good thing to send the king of England but only a bahar of cloves, which he hoped his majesty would accept in good part, considering his country yields no other thing of worth. Likewise he bestowed upon our general a bahar of cloves, and caused them presently to be carried to the boat; which done he took his leave, and departed aboard his caracoa.

The seventeenth day the king of Ternatè came rowing about our ship, and divers of his women with him, in a caracoa; the general entreating him to come aboard, but he would not. Kechil Gogogoe came aboard this afternoon to our general, certifying him that the contents of the Hollanders' counterfeit letter was, that we had sold powder, great ordnance, and other munition to the Portingals. And more, that to their great hurt in the fight we had assisted them

a later date. Meanwhile, some notice is due to the Ascension. The first attempt which we made to reach the Banda Islands was a failure. In pursuance of orders left by captain Lancaster on his departure from Bantam in 1603, a pinnace carrying some fifteen men, and laden with fifty-six chests and *fardels* of goods, was despatched for those islands on the sixth of March in that year. She met with contrary winds, and after *beating up and down in the seas* near two months, was forced to return to Bantam! The Ascension, as before stated, reached the place of her destination on the twentieth of February; but of the proceedings there we have no other information than what we gather from the letters written by James I. in reply to the sabandars of Nera and Lantore. It therein appears that captain Colthurst was received in a friendly manner, and that the sabandar of Nera, which is the principal island, sent his majesty a bahar of nutmegs.—E. Scott; *Appendix*.

with gunners, and that was the cause we left not a factory there, hoping the general would have carried and delivered it to his own disgrace; but he, suspecting their slanderous treachery, refused it.

The eighteenth day the king and his uncle came aboard in a small prāu, because he would not have the Hollanders, which rode by us, to know of his being there, for it was death to them to see him use our general kindly. Their coming was to take leave of our general. He desired them to come down to his cabin, and made them a banquet, which they kindly did accept, and spent most part of the day with him, urging our general to return thither again, or at the leastwise to send, and he or they should be welcome—do the Hollanders what they could; with protestation that both he and all his people were very sorry for his departure, finding we were good people, and not such as the Hollanders did report us to be, which lived only by robbing and stealing. During this communication the Holland ship which rode by us shot off three pieces, which the king hearing sent to know the cause. Word was brought the Hollanders' admiral was come from Tidorè, and gone aboard; which the king hearing, took a short farewell of our general and went to his caracoa—showing evidently his great fear to offend the Hollanders. Before he could put off his boat from the side our ship was under sail, giving him seven pieces of ordnance, and [we] held on our way between Ternatè and Tidorè.[154]

[154] *The Ascension.* "The one-and-twentieth day of July, being Sunday, we set sail from Banda, the wind at east-south-east, and we stood to the westward. The two-and-twentieth day we fell with the south end of Bouro, the wind at east-south-east. The seven-and-twentieth day we fell with *Deselem* [Salayer I.], and then we came about the south end of the island, leaving seven islands on our larboard side. We stood close by the wind to the northward, fair by the main island of *Deselem*, to clear ourselves of a small island and a shoal that lieth off the south-west part of *Deselem*, and leaving this island, and all the other shoals, on our larboard side, we stood north-north-west along the west side of *Deselem*, while we came in six degrees and ten minutes. Then we steered west eighteen

About noon the twenty-first day we came to an anchor at Taffasoa. The governor presently came to our general with a present of hens and fruit, telling him that he had been at Tidorè, and the king had given him order to surrender the town unto him if he came thither again, and the fort, praying him to dispose thereof as his own. The general gave him thanks, telling him he had few men; but if he had so many as he had when he came from Bantam, he would leave such a garrison there as they should doubt neither the Hollanders nor the Ternatans—but his weakness was such that he could leave no men there. He answered, he doubted not the keeping of the town in despite of all their enemies; and although he could leave no men there, yet had he order by his king to surrender his right and title to the king of England, to whose use he would keep it, desiring the surrender thereof might be drawn, and the general should have the original and he the copy. Which done, he caused the people to bring those cloves they had, and so took his leave and departed; we directing our course for Celebes, where we had such water as the place afforded—but it was brackish—buying some cocos of the people, who are like Javans.[155]

July the twenty-fourth we came to anchor in Bantam road,[156]

leagues, and fell with the point shoal that lieth off the south-west end of Celebes—and the very southernmost part of that shoal lieth in six degrees—and being clear of that, we stood to the westward. The sixteenth day of August, we came to anchor in Bantam road."—T. Clayborne.

155 I believe the previous narrative to be the *journal*, and that what follows, embracing a period of almost ten months, is the part which the publisher describes as a *continuation*. It contains, short as it is, two manifest errors. The writer contradicts himself as to the ship which accompanied the Hector, and asserts that Scott was left at Bantam! Scott and Clayborne may make amends for his defects: *they* wrote as eye-witnesses.

156 " The twenty-fourth of July our general came into the road from Tarnata. So soon as we discerned the ship, and saw it was the Dragon, I took a prāu, and went aboard to bid him welcome, who declared to me the dangers they had passed, and somewhat of the unkindness of the Hollanders, *etc.*—The twenty-fourth day the king of Jacatra [now Batavia] came to see our general.—The eighth of September the Dutch mer-

where master Scott, chief factor there, certified our general of the mortality of men in the Hector and Ascension [Susan] before they departed, so that he was forced to hire Chinese to help them home; and that of twenty-four left there in their factory twelve were dead. Where we continued till the sixth of October,[157] which day, having taken leave of master Scott and the rest left there, we set sail for England, continuing in our course with variable weather till the nineteenth of Decem-

chants invited our general and all his merchants and masters to a feast, where there was great cheer, and also great friendship was made between us.—The third day of October our general made a feast for his farewell, whereunto he invited the Dutch admiral, with also all the rest of his captains, masters, and merchants, where we were all exceeding merry, and great friendship was made between us.—The fourth day of October our general, being accompanied with divers merchants and others, went to the court to take his leave of the king and his nobles. The sixth day of October, being Sunday, about ten a-clock, our general with all that was bound home went aboard, who going by the Dutch house went in, and took his leave of the Dutch admiral and the rest of his merchants. Also there went aboard with him master Gabriel Towerson, who was to stay for agent there, and some other merchants who, after dinner, some went ashore, and some staid until the next day. About three a-clock we weighed anchor, and with some ordnance bade the town, and the Dutch ships, farewell. About eleven or twelve a-clock at night we came to an anchor under an island, where the next day we took in wood, which our general had sent men beforehand to cut ready. The seventh day, towards evening, we weighed anchor again, and set sail; master Towerson and some other of the merchants then took their leave to go ashore, whom we committed to the protection of the Almighty, and ourselves to the courtesy of the sea, desiring God to bless both them and us, and if it be his will to send us a happy meeting in England."—E. Scott.

157 *The Ascension.* "The sixth day of October, being Sunday, we set sail out of Bantam road, with the Dragon and the Ascension. The fifteenth day of November, latitude thirty-one degrees forty-eight minutes, the wind north-north-west, thick foggy weather. This day, about ten of the clock in the morning, we came within a ship's length of a rock, or sunken island. The water showed upon it very brown and muddy, and in some places very blue, and being a ship's breadth or two to the northward of it, we saw the water by the ship's side very black and thick, as though it had been earth or gross sand boiling up from it. The variation in this place is one-and-twenty degrees from north to west decreasing."—T. Clayborne.

ber,— which day, the wind scanting upon us,[158] we thought to put into Saldanha road.[159] About ten a-clock in the morning we saw a sail to leewards, thinking it had been the Ascension, whose company we lost fourteen days before, but contrary to our expectation it proved the Hector, which went in company of the Susan from Bantam above nine months before, in such lamentable distress that, had we not met with them that day, they had purposed the next to have run themselves aground at Penguin Island, having for that purpose fardled up their apparel[160] and such other things as were most necessary for them. Our general caused our pinnace to be hoisted out, and sent for captain Keeling and the purser, who related their extreme miseries, having but ten

[158] The *wind scanting.* The phrase, misinterpreted by Todd, has a technical sense—as in this example: "the wind *scanting* with us, and *larging* with them, we were forced to leeward."—Sir R. Hawkins.

[159] *The Ascension.* "The sixteenth of December, west nine leagues, latitude thirty-four degrees and twenty minutes. This day, in the morning, we had sight of the land of *Ethiopia* [South Africa], distant from us some twelve leagues. The six-and-twentieth day latitude thirty-four degrees thirty minutes. Now, being in the latitude and in the sight of Cape Boa Esperança, and within one league of it, we steered north-west, and north-north-west, and north, and as the land lay about the cape. The seven-and-twentieth day we came to anchor in Saldanha road, where we found our admiral, and the Hector, which ship, the Dragon our admiral met withal seven days before, driving up and down the sea about four leagues off the Cape Boa Esperança with ten men in her. All the rest of her men were dead, which were in number three-and-fifty which died since she came out of Bantam, which time was nine months. Being in great distress, she lost company of the Susan three months after she came out of Bantam road, which ship, the Susan, was never heard of since. Here we came to anchor in seven fathoms, having the low point going in north-west-by-west, and the Sugar-Loaf south-west, half-a-point to the westward, the point of the breach of Penguin Island north-west-by-north, and the hill between the Sugar-Loaf and the low point west-south-west, the peak of the hill to the eastward of the Table south-by-east."—T. Clayborne.

[160] *Fardled up their apparel.* Johnson omits *fardle* as a verb. It was, however, in common use. *Fardle,* in a nautical sense, is the undoubted origin of *furl.*—Capt. Smith.

Englishmen and four Chinese alive; so, supper being done, with thanks given to God for their miraculous preservation, our general sent twelve men more to help them into Saldanha road, where we staid repairing the ruins of the Hector and providing other necessaries till the sixteenth of January following [1606], when we set sail for Saint Helena,[161] where we arrived the second of February following.

161 *The Ascension.* "The sixteenth day of January [1606], in the morning, we set sail from Saldanha road, and went to the northward of Penguin Island, between that and the main. When we had the island south from us about one-mile-and-a-half we sounded, and had ground twenty fathoms, white coral and *whistles* of shells. When we were clear of the island we stood off west-by-south and west-south-west, while we brought the island south-east-by-east of us; now, being about six of the clock in the afternoon, we had sight of the Hector, coming out to the southward of the island, for we left her at anchor when we weighed. Now the wind being at south, we stood all night to the westward, close by a wind. In the morning following we had lost sight of the Hector and then we steered away north-west with a low sail while [till?] noon, being the seventeenth day, thinking to get sight of the Hector, but we could not. The first day of February, west to the southward sixteen leagues, of latitude sixteen degrees and twenty minutes. This day, about one of the clock in the afternoon, we had sight of Saint Helena, bearing west to the northward from us about twelve or thirteen leagues. The second day west, and west-by-south, four leagues, then having the island west from us about eight or nine leagues, the wind at south-east, we lay off and on to the eastward of the island most part of the night, and in the morning following we stood to the northward of the island. This day, about twelve of the clock, we came to anchor in the road of Saint Helena. Our land-anchor lay in seventeen fathoms; our ship rode in twenty fathoms, blackish, gravelly sand. We had one point north-east of us, and one sharp hill like a sugar-loaf, with a cross on the top of it, that bare north-east-by-east. The church in the valley south-east. In this valley there are many trees likewise: the high land south-east up from the church, and all the valley besides, is full of trees. The other point of the land, south-west to the westward. We moored south-east and north-west. Our anchor in the offing lay in one-and-twenty fathoms. The third day at night, being Monday, we had sight of the Hector, coming about the south end of the island, but could not fetch into the road, yet stood to the northward as near as she could lie, the wind at east. The fourth and fifth days, our boats went out to help to get her into the road, but they could not. The sixth day at night, being

The eleventh of February we departed from Saint Helena, continuing at sea with such variety of weather as those that use the sea are usually accustomed unto till the second of May following, when we were off Plymouth, and the sixth following at the Downs.

a little wind, we towed her in with our boats into thirty-five fathoms, one-mile-and-a-half from the shore, bearing from us south-west-by-west, distant about two leagues. The eleventh day we set sail from Saint Helena, the wind at east-north-east, and we steered north-west. This north-west part of the island lieth in the latitude of sixteen degrees, and in seven degrees forty-five minutes of variation. Note this, that the church that bare south-east of us when we were in the road, standeth in the bottom of the fifth valley from that point that bare north-east of us. We came to anchor in the Downs on the sixth of May 1606, where we rode eight days for a fair wind."—T. Clayborne.

FINIS.

THE KING OF TARNATA, TO THE KING OF ENGLAND, SCOTLAND, FRANCE AND IRELAND, &C.[162]

HEARING of the good report of your Maiestie, by the comming of the great captain Francis Drake, in the time of my father, which was about some 30. yeeres past: by the which captaine, my predecessor did send a ring vnto the Queene of England, as a token of remembrance betweene vs: which if the aforesaide Drake had beene liuing, hee could haue informed your Maiestie of the great loue and friendship of either side: he in the behalfe of the Queene: my father for him and his successors. Since which time of the departure of the aforesaid captaine, we haue dayly expected his returne, my father liuing many yeeres after and dayly expecting his returne, and I after the death of my father haue liued in the same hope, till I was father of eleuen children: in which time I haue beene informed that the English were men of so bad disposition that they came not as peaceable merchants, but to dispossesse them of their countrey: which by the comming of the bearer hereof wee haue found to the contrarie, which greatly we reioyce at. And after many yeeres of our

[162] This interesting letter, and the two which follow it, are printed LITERATIM from the former edition, as favourable specimens of the volume in point of orthography and punctuation. The variations of the manuscript copies preserved at the India-House, with which they have been collated, are of no importance. The *bezoar stones* sent by the king of Bantam—articles, says Bullokar, "very costly and of great account in physic"—were delivered to his majesty on the 25th May 1606. The letters of James I. which produced the above letters, with those written in reply, are printed in the Appendix.—*India-House* Mss.; *English expositor.*

expectation of some English forces by the promise of captaine Drake, here arriued certaine ships which we well hoped had beene Englishmen, but finding them contrary, and being out of al hope of succour of the English nation, we were inforced to write to the Prince of Holland, to craue ayde and succour against our auncient enemies the Portingals, and according to our request hee hath sent hither his forces which hath expeld all the Portugales out of the fortes which they held at Amboyna and Tydore. And whereas your Maiestie hath sent to me a most kinde and friendly letter by your seruant captaine Henry Middleton, that doth not a litle reioyce vs.

And whereas captaine Henry Middelton was desirous to leaue a factory heare, we were very willing therunto, which the captain of the Hollanders vnderstanding, he came to challenge me of a former promise which I had written to the Prince of Holland: that if he would send me such succour as should expell the Portugales out of these parts, that no other nation should haue trade heare but they onely. So that we were inforst against our liking to yeeld vnto the Hollanders captaines request for this time: whereof we craue pardon of your Highnesse: and if any of your nation come hereafter, they shall be welcome. And whereas the chiefe captaine of the Hollanders doth sollicite vs, not to hold any friendship with your nation, nor to giue eare to your Highnesse letters: yet for all their suite, if you please to send hither againe, you shall be welcome. And in token of our friendship, which we desire of your Maiestie, we haue sent you a small remembrance of a bahar of cloues, our countrey being poore, and yeelding no better commoditie, which we pray your Highnesse to accept in good part.

TARNATA.

THE KING OF TYDORS LETTER TO THE KINGS MAIESTIE OF ENGLAND.

THIS writing of the King of Tydor to the King of England, is to let your Highnesse vnderstand that the King of Holland hath sent hither into these partes a fleet of shippes to ioyne with our ancient enemie the King of Tarnata, and they ioyntly together, haue ouer-runne and spoyled part of our countrey, and are determined to destroy both vs and our subiects. Nowe vnderstanding by the bearer hereof, captaine Henry Middleton, that your Highnesse is in frienship with the King of Spaine, wee desire your Maiestie that you would take pittie of vs, that wee may not be destroyed by the King of Holland and Tarnata to whom wee haue offered no wrong: but they by forceable meanes seeke to bereaue vs of our kingdome. And as great kings vpon the earth are ordayned by GOD *to succour all them that be wrongfully oppressed: so I appeale vnto your Maiestie, for succour against my enemies; not doubting but to finde reliefe at your Maiesties hands. And if your Maiestie send hither, I humbly entreate that it may bee captaine Henry Middleton or his brother, with whom I am well acquainted.*

Thus we end, praying GOD *to enlarge your kingdomes, and blesse you, and all your counsels.*

TYDOR.

THE KING OF BANTAM, TO THE KING OF ENGLAND.

A LETTER giuen from your friend the King of Bantam, to the King of England, Scotland, France, and Ireland: desiring GOD *to preserue your health, and to exalt you more and more, and all your counsell. And whereas your Maiestie hath sent a generall, Henry Middleton, he came to me in health. I did heare that your Maiestie was come to the crowne of England, which doth greatly reioyce my heart. Now England and Bantam are both as one. I haue also receiued a present from your Maiestie: the which I giue you many thankes for your kindnesse. I doe send your Maiestie two beasar stones, the one waying fourteene masses the other three: and so* GOD *haue you in his keeping.*

BANTAM.

APPENDIX.

[No. I.—Commission of James I. authorising Henry Middleton esquire, and, in case of his decease, Christopher Colthurst gentleman, *to use and put in execution* martial law. 1604.]

Decima-octava pars Pateñ de anno Regni Regis Jacobi Primo. (*m.* 33 *dorso.*)

Coñ spial p Mecatorib; de le East Indies.

James by the grace of God etc. To our trustie and welbeloved Henry Middleton esquier and to our trustie and welbeloved Christofer Colthurst gentleman greeting Whereas divers of our loving subjects at their owne adventures costs and charges aswell for the honor of this oure realme of England as for the increase and advancement of trade of marchandize within the same did heretofore sett forth a voyage to the Easte Indies with certayne shippes and pynnaces by way of marchandizing by which shippes and pynnaces they having discovered and begon to settle a trade in some partes of the said East Indies and their shippes being retorned from thence laden with sundrie marchandize brought from those partes they the said marchants intending to frequent those countries of the East Indies by contynuing the trade already discovered and begonne and indevoring further discovery of trade of those partes for the more ample vent of the native com'odities of oure kingdomes and retornyng from the places of their discovery of such necessarie com'odities as shalbe of speciall use and benefytt both to us and our subjects are in hand to prepare and make ready their said shippes lately retorned from the East Indies and to set them forth agayne for a newe voyage And whereas the said marchants have chosen you the said Henry Middleton to be the principall governor or generall and you the said Christofer Colthurst to be lieutenant generall of all the marchants marryners and other our subjects which are or shalbe shipped in any of the said shippes wee graciouslie favoring their intended voyage and approving and allowing of their choice of you to the same goverment being desirous to furnish you with all fytt and convenient power and authority to rule and governe all and every our subjects imployed in this voyage by a due obedience to be by them yeilded unto you in the observing and executing of all such good orders and constituc'ons as you shall thinke convenient to ordayne and appoynt for the furtherance of the said voyage to the honor of us and oure kingdomes and for the advancement of the said trade WEE DOE HEREBY straightly charge and comaunde all and every person and persons imployed used or shipped or which shalbe imployed used or shipped in this voyage in any of the said shippes to give all due obedience and respect unto you during the said voyage and to beare them selves therein one towards another in all good order and quietnes for avoyding any occasion that might breede mutynye quarrells or dissention amongest them to the hynderance of the good successe which is to be hoped for by Gods providence of the saide intended voyage and in default of such dutie and obedience to be performed towards you and for the correcc'on and quenching of all such muteny quarrells or dissention that shall or may growe or be moved by the disorder evill disposic'on or perversenes of any of the said persons WEE DOE HEREBY authorize you Henry Middleton generall during the said voyage or during soe longe tyme as you shall live in the same voyage and in case of your decease (which God forbid) wee doe then likewise hereby authorize you the saide Christofer Colthurst to chastice correct and punysh all offendors and transgressors in that behalfe according to the quality of their offences with such punishments as are com'only used in all armies by sea when the offences are not capitall and for capitall offences as wilfull murder which is hatefull in the sight of God or muteny which is an offence that may tende to the overthrowe of the said voyage the same being truly and justly proved against any of the person or persons aforesaid wee doe hereby give unto you the said Henry Middleton duryng all the tyme of the said voyage or duryng soe longe tyme as you shall live in the same and in case of your decease wee doe give to you Christofer Cothurst full power and authoritie to use and put in execuc'on oure lawe called marciall lawe in that behalfe and theis our l'res shalbe your sufficient warrant and discharge for the doyng and executing of all and singuler the premisses AND FORASMUCH as at this present tyme wee are in amitye with all Christian princes and are unwilling that any of oure subjects should give occasion of breche or hinderance of that league or amytie which wee hold with any oure confederates frendes or allies and because wee are not ignorant of the emulac'on and envy that doth accompany the discovery of countries and trades and of the quarrells and contencions which doe many tymes fall oute betwene the subjects of divers princes that meete the one with the other in forreyn and farre remote countries in the course and prosecuting of their discoveries and being desirous that oure subjects should forbeare to move or begyn any quarrell or contencion uppon the subjects of any of oure confederates frendes or alyes either in the proceeding or retorne uppon or from any of their voyages WEE THEREFORE doe hereby straightlie charge and com'aunde you Henry Middleton and you Christofer Colthurst and all others under your goverment that neither in your voyage outeward or homeward nor in any conntry iland port or place where you shall abide or come during the tyme of your being abroad oute of oure kingdomes or domynions where you may meete with any the subjects of the king of Spayne or of any other oure confederates frendes or alyes their shippes vessells goodes or marchandize you doe attempt or goe about to sett uppon take or surprise their persons shippes vessells goodes or marchandize or offer any injurye or discurtesie unto them unles you shall first by them thereunto justly be provoked or driven in the juste defence of your owne persons your shippes vessells goodes or marchandizes as you will answere to the contrary at your uttermost perills. IN WITNES whereof etc. WITNES our selfe at Westmynster the third day of March.

P' bre' de privato sigillo etc.

RECORD OFFICE.
Nov. 19.
1850.

This is a true and authentic copy from the original record remaining in the Chapel of the Rolls having been examined.

THOMAS PALMER,
Ass^t. Record Keeper.

19 November 1850.

[No. II.—Commission of James I. authorising the East-India Company to export the value of £12,000 in foreign coin. 1604.]

Quinta-decima pars Pateñ de Anno Regni Regis Jacobi Primo.

Đ Liceñ spāł ꝑ Gub̄natore ⁊ Societāt Mēcatoꝝ de le East Indies.

James by the grace of God etc. To all men to whome theise p'esentes shall come greetynge Wheareas our late deare sister Elizabeth by her l'res patents under the greate seale of England bearing date at Westm' the one and thirtith day of December in the three and fortith year of her raigne did uppon peticion made unto her by her deare and lovinge cosen George earle of Cumb'land and divers other her welbeloved subjects for her royall assent and licence to be graunted unto them that they at their owne adventure costs and charges aswell for the honor of this realme of England as for the increase of navigation and advancement of trade of merchandize within the same mighte adventure and sett fourthe certayne voyages with a convenient nomber of shippes and pynnaces by waie of traffique and merchandize into the East Indies in the countries and parts of Asia and Affrica did incorporate the saide petitioners into a bodie politique by the name of the governour and companie of the marchaunts of London tradinge into the East Indies to have houlde and enjoy the sole benefit of the trade and trafficque of the saide Easte Indies for the space of fifteene yeares from the birth of our Lord God then last paste before the date of the said l'res patents And whereas by the saide l'res patents licence is graunted to the saide governour and companie of marchaunts of London tradinge into the East Indies to t'ansporte oute of this realme into the saide Indies in everie of their voyages duringe the saide tearme of fifteene yeares all such forreine coyne of silver Spanishe or other forreyn silver or bullion of silver as they shall duringe the saide tearme bringe or cause to be broughte into this realme of England from the parts beyond the seas either in the same kynde sorte stampe or fashion which it shall have when they brynge it in or anie other forme stampe or fashion to be coyned in the mynte within the Tower of London soe as the whole quantyties of coyne or monies by them to be transported in anie their saide voyages duringe the saide terme doe not exceede the value of thirtie thousand poundes in any one voiage and soe as the som'e of six thousand poundes at the leaste parcell of the same som'e or value of thirtie thousande poundes soe to bee transported as aforesaide be first coyned within the saide Tower of London before the same shalbee transported in anie the saide voyages as by the saide l'res patents more at large appeareth Nowe forasmuch as the saide governour and company of the saide marchants since the saide l'res patents to them granted have made one voyage into the saide East Indies and retourned their shippes from thence laden with sondry kinds of marchandize and have alsoe prepared and are readie to set forth another voiage into the saide East Indies and they the saide governor and company being desirous and endevouring by all good meanes to manage and carry their said trade as neere as they can rather by the t'ansportac'on of the native com'odities of our kingdomes and by the bartering and exchange of them for forren com'odities then by using the benefit granted them by the said l'res patents for the carying out of so much tresure in every of their voiages doe content themselves in this p'esent voyage with the lib'ty of t'ansportac'on of twelve thousand pounds in forrein coyne without t'ansportac'on of anie other coyne bulloyn or silver and to that end have made humble peticyon unto us that they may t'ansport the saide value of twelve thousand pounds of forreyn coine without coyning the same or anie part thereof in our mynt within our Tower of London the rather for that they found by experience in their last voiage that they could not without great difficulty and some losse to the said marchants in the value of their monies newe coyned for that voiage make trade for their marchandize in the said East Indies because the said mony being stamped with the ymage and sup'scripc'on of our said deare sister was strange and unknowne to the people of those parts and the monies nowe to [be] coyned in our said mint being to be coined with a new stamp of our owne ymage and sup'scripc'on will nott only draw them into the like hindrance in their trade when they shall come into the saide Indies but will cause their shipps which are nowe allmoste ready to depart in their voiage to stay and to be detained here to their further damage and hindrance untill new stamps for the coyning of the said monies in our mynt shalbe graven and made for that purpose WEE THEREFORE favouring the saide marchants and being desirous to give themall furtherance and expedic'on in their p'esent intended voiage of our esp'iall grace ce'ten knowledge and mere moc'on have granted and by theis p'esents for us our heires and successors doe grant unto the said governor and company of marchants tradyng into the East Indies that it shall and may bee lawfull for them their factors and assignes in thys p'esent intended voiage which is prepared or in p'eparing for the second voiage into the said East Indies to t'ansport out of this our realme of England all such forreyn coyne or silver either Spanish or other forrein silver as they have prepared p'cured or gotten or shall prepare p'cure or gett being alreadie broughte or to be broughte from the parts beyond the seas before the dep'ting of their shipps out of the river of Thames so as the wholl quantity of the coyne and monies by them to be t'ansported in this their p'esent intended voyage being the second voyage toward the saide Indies doe not exceed the saide value of twelve thousand pounds the same to be t'ansported in the same kinde sort stampe or fashion as the said moneys is or shalbe p'cured gotten or broughte into this realme of England and that withoute anie newe coyning or alte'ing of the said monies or anie parte thereof from the stampe which it beareth ANIE statute restraint or p'hibic'on in that behalf to the cont'ary in any wise notwithstanding. IN WITNES whereof etc. WITNES our self at Westm' the xxiijth day of February.

P' bre' de privato sigillo etc.

RECORD OFFICE.
Nov. 19.
1850.

This is a true and authentic copy from the original record remaining in the Chapel of the Rolls having been examined.

THOMAS PALMER,
Asst. Record Keeper.

19 November 1850.

[No. III.—A Commission of the governor, the deputy, and the committees of the East-India Company; being the instructions for master Henry Middleton and others employed in their second voyage to the East-Indies. 1604.][1]

A Commission set down by us the Governor, the Deputy, and Committees of the *East-India* Company, to our loving friends, master *Henrie Middleton*, general of the merchants, mariners, and others employed by us in this present intended voyage, being our second voyage to the *East Indies;* and to master *Christofer Colthurst*, master *Roger Style*, master *William Kealinge*, and masters our principal merchants and factors in the said voyage, and every of them respectively, as the directions and instructions of this our present commission may concern their several places of trust wherein they are employed—the which voyage, Almighty God in his mercy make prosperous.

Whereas we have, upon a special conceit of your wisdom, discretion, and good government, made choice of you, master *Henrie Middleton*, to be principal governor and general of our fleet, and have submitted to your command the persons of all the merchants, mariners, and others employed in the several ships thereof; which ships we have fitted and furnished with all necessaries not only meet for the voyage, but such as you could require, or wish to be supplied with your full contentment.

We therefore expect, on your part, such a performance and

[[1] This important and instructive document is preserved among the India-House Mss.—It is printed verbatim; but, with the exception of proper names, and words of dubious sense, in modernised orthography.]

1 The Company's inducement to make choice of these persons.

carrying of this government committed to your charge as may not only confirm us in that hope and good conceit which induced us to the choice of you to this employment, but may add unto yourself an increase and advancement of your own reputation ; which, no doubt, you may effect, observing this moderation in your said government, so to command as you may be both loved and feared, not using authority to work your private respect or revenge, but studying and endeavouring to bring this long and tedious voyage to a profitable end, with care of the safety, health, and comfort of your people, and using your industry to recompense so great a charge of provisions and other burdens and expenses borne in this voyage, with a profitable return to the general state of the Company.

2 To use the assistance of certain nominated.

And that you may the better proceed in an infallible hope of a good issue of your endeavours, we wish and exhort you first to depend confidently upon God's providence, and next, propound to yourself the good example of your late predecessor, sir *James Lancaster*, in the carrying of the former voyage. And forasmuch as no man is so absolute in his course and directions for the managing of any occasions of importance but he may therein receive light, and especial help and furtherance, by conference with others; therefore we have, for your assistance and help, the better to undergo the charge of our business, made choice of master *Christofer Colthurst*, master *Roger Style*, master *William Keeleing*, master *Robert Browne*, and master *Edward Highlord*, as our principal merchants employed in this voyage, to be ready with their advice and aid to assist you in any thing that may belong to the same; whom we pray and require you not only to hear, but lovingly and kindly to use and respect, so as, by your kind conversation mutually used and had, the one with the other, there may grow between you in so firm an unity as shall be subject to no jar or distaste ; wherein, if you link together, all things will pass with felicity and contentment : otherwise, if there fall amongst you envy, emulation, or disagreement, there is no hope of good success of the voyage, but apparent hazard to the overthrow of the same. And this shall suffice for our general advice unto you for such a moderation of government, to be performed on your part, as may breed a good affection towards you in those that are submitted unto your command.

And to the end that the whole company committed to your

charge may perform that due obedience and respect unto you which is fit to be yielded to their governor or general, we do herein propound unto you the care of the due execution of that principal mean which draweth all Christians to conformity and submission to such as are set over them—which is the daily invocation and religious worship and service of God—requiring you to take order that certain hours and times in every day may be set apart for public prayer and calling upon the name of God; that like orders, with penalties, to be severally published and set up in every ship, against the blaspheming of the name of God, and all idle and filthy communication; that all unlawful gaming, especially dice-play, may be abolished, as that which procureth, not only the blaspheming of the name of God, but envy and quarrelling, from whence many times proceedeth murders, or, at the least, the impoverishing and undoing of many of the poor ungoverned mariners, who by the liberty of dice-play lose their whole wages of the voyage, as it is not unknown unto you by the practice of divers in the last voyage, who to furnish themselves with money in that unthrifty employment engaged themselves to pay three for one upon their return; and thus having wasted their wages by such unthrifty means, went about to lay a scandal upon the Company, alleging they were oppressed by necessity in the voyage to enter into those excessive, usurious contents [sic] to maintain their lives.

3 Daily prayers to be used by the whole company.

You having thus set an order to be observed in every ship, both for the service of God and the civil behaviour of the company amongst themselves—then, for the better assistance, strength, and comfort that the whole fleet may take one of another, by keeping company together throughout the whole voyage, until you come into the *East Indies*, into the port or haven of *Bantam*, where you are to take order with the masters and company of every ship, by the best observations and directions which you shall in your conference together agree upon, that you depart not out of sight one of another so long as you may possibly keep together, to the end that if any of you should be any way distressed upon any occasion, you may be relieved and comforted by the assistance of some of your consorts not being far off. And if you shall happen to be separated by foul weather, and cannot recover the sight one of another in short time, if your separation or dispersing happen to be before you come to island of *May* [Maio], then let that island be the place of your repair or rendezvous, that you may be drawn

4 To keep company one with another.

again together in company, and there to stay one for another seven or eight days; and having made stay there so long, and the company missing not being come thither, then to depart forwards on the voyage, leaving some apparent mark behind you that you have been at the said island—as by raising some heap of stones together, setting up of a stake or mark, and leaving there some letter in or near the place, which may be found by them as shall come after, whereby they may know that the other ship or ships are past that place. And if your separation be beyond the island of *May*, then your rendezvous to be at the island of *St. Lawrence* [Madagascar]. And if you shall be occasioned to land in any place for fresh water, or to refresh your men, it shall behove you to keep

5 Warlike guard to be kept in watering or refreshing men, etc.

good order and discipline, by warlike guard, for the safety of your company, lest they should be surprised and fall into danger by over much confidence and security; and, the safety of your persons being provided for, then your whole company to be admonished to behave themselves peaceably and civilly towards the people of that place where you refresh for the supply of your wants; and that they be also exhorted to a moderation in feeding off fruits and fresh victuals of that soil, the which, by their intemperate and immoderate diet, may breed inconveniences formerly found by experience to be the loss of many men's lives. And in such place or places of refreshing, you shall do well to give special order to some men chosen and appointed to that end, to make the general provision, both of fresh victuals and fruit, for the whole fleet, whereby an equal repartition thereof may be made for the company of every ship, and that every one be not, with limitation, to victual himself according to his intemperate appetite; and this order to be taken, prohibiting every person, upon pain of severe punishment, that they do not range and straggle after fresh victuals and fruits, but by such order as shall be prescribed unto them.

6 Refreshing by landing not to be used upon light occasion.

Upon such opportunities of necessary landing of your people for refreshing, which by no means we would have otherwise to be used upon light occasion, for that it will greatly hinder the voyage, we do require you to give order unto the preacher to prepare himself to preach to the people, being come together out of the several ships, making his choice of such fit arguments and places of Scripture as may be most agreeable to the time and occasion, whereby the whole company may be exhorted and taught the better to carry themselves in the general business. And that the preacher may have the more comfort in his ministry, we pray you be careful that all due respects be given him, not only by yourself, but by the whole company, that his doctrine and exhortations, by contempt or neglect of his ministry, return not without profit. For the place of your refreshing, we wish it to be the island of *St. Lawrence,* but not at *Saldania* [Saldanha] in anywise, for the inconveniences of that island [bay] noted unto us by men of good experience, and their caution given us to beware of the danger of that place; wherefore we require you to shun this place, as our express order and will herein. 7

To go thence to *Bantam*, and to dispose of business.

Your refreshing place being left, and all opportunities taken for the admonishing of your people, both to the service of God, without which no enterprise can be prosperous, and to the civil and orderly carrying of themselves in the voyage, and in all service thereto belonging, then you are to shape your course directly for *Bantam* aforesaid; at which port, as soon as you shall arrive, and that you may conveniently draw yourselves together in conference with master *William Starkey,* [or] the agent which you shall find there succeeding him in the business, then we do require you (as God hath guided and brought you to your expected and appointed port, where you may enter into the disposing of your business) that then, you being come to the merchandising port of the voyage, you do proceed therein as followeth, viz.: 8

To advise and confer of the state of the place, usage, and all other circumstances.

We do will and require you, master *Henrie Middleton,* our governor or general of the whole voyage, and you, master *Christofer Colthurst,* master *Roger Style,* master *William Kealinge,* master *Robert Browne,* and master *Edward Highlorde,* our principal merchants for the disposing of the merchandises and traffic of your said voyage, that you advise and confer together with master *William Starkey,* or with whomsoever standeth in the place of the agent resident at *Bantam,* of the state of the place, and of the usage that our agent and factors have received since they were left there, and of all other circumstances that may concern the safety and benefit of the trade; which being found to stand in good terms, then you are to deliver our letters to our said agent, and, with his advice, to deliver the king's majesty's letters and present to the king of that place, and then to land all such monies as are laden in our four several ships, viz., 11,160*li.* 12*s.*, in royals-of-eight, whereof in the Red Dragon

DRAGON, five chests, cont. 4,000*li.* in royals, in 40 bags.

9 To land monies.

HECTOR, four chests, cont. 3,200 *li.* in royals, in 32 bags.

ASCENSION, three chests, cont. 2,400 *li.* in royals, in 24 bags.

SUSAN, two chests, cont. 1,560$\frac{3}{5}$ *li.* in royals, in 15 bags.

Which being done, then to take information from the agent of the state of our business left in his charge, what quantity of lading he hath in a readiness for the ships, causing the dust to be sift from the pepper, if it be not done already, upon advice given that end by our former letters; for which purpose we send with you garblers with sieves and fans, to the end that our ships should not be discharged with unprofitable commodities.

10 Garblers sent.

11 What commodities fit, and what provided at the *Molloccos.*

To take like information what commodities, and how much lading is provided at the *Molloccos* [Malucos], conferring with our said agent what ships of our fleet are fittest to go for the *Molloccos*, remembering that the Hector and Ascension are victualled for twenty-four months. The experience of our said factors, gained by their long abode at *Bantam*, will well inform you how to proceed in the sending of our shipping to the *Molloccos*, and for the ordering of the merchandise for that place.

12 The ships laden, and sent from *Bantam* for *England*, who is to go to the *Molloccos*, and to what end.

The provision for the lading at *Bantam* being laden aboard our ships that are first to return for *England*, and the commanders thereof shipped in the said ships, and those ships prepared ready, which by you and the agents shall be resolved upon to go for the *Mollocos*, our direction is, that you, master *Henrie Middleton*, to go yourself in one of the said ships, to the *Molloccos*, taking with you such of our factors to leave to reside in the *Molloccos*, and such stock for their maintenance, as you shall, upon conference together at *Bantam*, agree upon to remain in their hands for the maintenance of them and the residue which are already resident at *Bantam* by their abode there; in which space they may both learn the language of the country, and dispatch such business as they shall be by you appointed unto. And we wish you to take with you to *Banda*, one or both of the garblers, with their instruments and provisions to cleanse the cloves from dust and stalks, and the nutmegs from rumps and dust, that our ships be not pestered with the dust or garble of these kinds of commodities.

13 No particular trade, etc.; penalties, loss of the commodities laden, except, etc.

And for that the voyage of this condition and great charge cannot admit any private trade, our will is, that neither yourself nor any others, upon any particular, or other account than the general and joint stock, do lade, or be permitted to lade, any of these commodities in our ships, viz.: pepper, cloves, mace, nutmegs, China-silk, indigo, ambergris, musk, civet, bezoar stones, camphor, benjamin, *buxrace* or cinnamon; but that what quantity soever of these commodities may be had or brought up, shall be laden for the joint account of the Company, upon pain of the loss of every such commodity so laden, and not laden upon the joint account. But if, upon license demanded of you, the said general, and you our said principal merchants, any master, mariner, or others, shall be desirous to lade some small proportion or quantity of China-dishes, or light trifles, not exceeding the value of three pounds, or not bearing above the bulk of a small chest—then we do order, that all such goods, so laden by your privity and license, shall be entered into the purser's book of such ship wherein the same is laden, to the end that if any of them do die by the way, their friends may enjoy that which is theirs according to their wills.

14 What goods left in the *East Indies*, since bought, etc., what monies and debts, etc.

And for the better remembrance and instruction of you the said general, and of you the principal merchants, what goods were left behind at *Bantam*, in the coming away of sir *James Lancaster* out of the *Indies*, and what hath been provided since by the agent there, as by their advice sent us since the coming home of our ships may appeare, you shall understand that sir *James Lancaster* left at *Bantam* above 1,500 bags of pepper; and by their letters sent from *Bantam* by the Dutch ships, the agent wrote that he had provided 1,500 bags more. And after, sir *James* gave commission to the agent, at his departure from *Bantam*, that if the Dutchmen were disposed to buy any of the Company's pepper, and would give good profit for it, that then the agent should sell it, and provide more for the Company at better opportunity and better rate; upon which commission so left, you may inquire what hath been done for the benefit of the Company. It doth also appear by the abbreviate of the accounts sent home out of the *Indies*, that there remained in the hands of the agent, master *Starkey*, 482 fardels of calicos, viz.: 8 canisters of pintados, and 117 fardels of checkered stuffs, 51 fardels of long *malow* girdles, 59 fardels of girdles for *Sysan*, 110 fardels of *Java* girdles, 13 chests of fine pintados, 6 chests of divers sorts of commodities, 42 fardels of brown calicos, and in loose pintados, by estimate made by sir *James Lancaster*, about 80 fardels at the least, of all sorts; so that there might be in all, packs and canisters, about 482 fardels, as aforesaid; and in loose calicos, so [say] 30 fardels; so as there appeareth in the whole to be 512 fardels. Since the departure of our ships, we understand, by their letters of the 15th of February 1602 [1603], they had shipped [52 fardels] for *Banda* in the *Molloccos,* aboard our pinnace—which, we trust, arrived there in safety within short time after her departure from *Bantam*—upon the proceeds of which 52 fardels, it is hoped by us that there may be sufficient, with a large overplus, to lade the two ships we have appointed to the *Molloccos* with mace, cloves, and nutmegs; so that there remained, after the departure of the pinnace from *Bantam,* 452 fardels, or thereabouts, containing the best and richest commodities of the whole complement of the prize—the other 52 fardels sent to the *Molloccos* being of the meanest and basest kinds of the said prize goods: which great remainder of goods at *Bantam,* of the best and greatest value, cannot but upon the proceeds thereof, readie before your arrival at *Bantam,* [occasion] great quantities of commodities to be returned from thence.

Besides all which several quantities of goods before mentioned, there remained in the hands of master *Starkey* and the rest, at the departure of the ships homewards, 4,907 royals-of-eight, and in debts 3,941 pieces-of-eight, being compassed in the same 77 bags of pepper, which pepper was received into their custody; so as if all the goods and money left with them, and that which might and hath proceeded thereof, do rest in safety, you shall not only have sufficient to lade your four ships with pepper, mace, cloves, and nutmegs, but as many more ships of the like burden, besides the monies which you carry along with you in the ships, amounting to 11,160$\frac{3}{8}$*li.* 12*s.* [sic] in royals, as aforesaid; which monies, because you know that spices are here of no value, we wish you to employ in some other commodities that may be of more estimation and yield a better profit—as raw silk, well chosen, and bought at reasonable prices, or such like commodities, wherewith these parts of Christendom have not been glutted, as with spices.

15 The 11,160*li.* 12*s.* to be employed, not in spices, but in other commodities more profitable.

16 The 11,160*li.* 12*s.* not to be mixed in account with the former adventure, and cause why.

And touching the said 11,160$\frac{3}{8}$*li.* in royals, now sent in these ships, for so much as it is a new supply of stock, sent out upon a new adventure, we will not have the same to be mixed in account with the former adventure, but do require you to keep the account of the employment hereof alone by itself. And to the end that the same may be distinguished from the former accounts of the first adventure, we do pray and require you, the said general and principal merchants, by conference and assistance of the factors resident both at *Bantam* and *Banda,* to make a valuation, as near as you can, of all the remainder of the first stock, what it may be worth to be sold; for that many of the adventurers who are unwilling to hang and continue long in accounts imperfect and undetermined, are desirous to sell their remainders of their stock to such as will continue the trade; and therefore a valuation is to be conceived, and sent with the return of these ships, at any hand, being a matter not only desired by the generality, but expressly agreed upon and charged upon us that have the ordering of the business, to see it performed; which charge being not in us to perform, we lay upon you, in whose power the performance thereof lieth, as you will answer the neglect thereof.

17 What master *Starkey* hath besides the former goods, etc., left at *Bantam*.

Besides the former particulars of prize goods and monies before mentioned, there appeareth further to rest in the hands of master *Starkey* and the other factors, ten pieces of cloths of divers colours, containing 514 English yards; a basin and ewer of silver, poiz. 102 oz.; two standing cups, poiz. 63 oz.—whereof they are to give you an account at your being at *Bantam*.

18 What wood is to be provided.

If those parts of the *Indies* do yield any good quantity of ebony, *ffarnando bucke* [Pernambuco], or such like heavy wood of value, you may provide so much thereof as will ballast your ships, so that the same take up no room of stowing that may otherwise be more profitably employed.

19 To prevent the *Portingalls'* malice; and what is to be carried to the *Mollocos*.

And forasmuch as we are not ignorant that the malice of the *Portingalls* towards our discovery of the trade to those parts, will not let him abstain from all practices of annoyance which lieth in his power to offer and perform to the trade of the *Mollocos*, who happily may, by some lying of wait for the intercepting of our pinnace sent to *Banda*, deprive us of the provisions which otherwise that voyage might supply us withal—if any such or other preventing accident hath happened, yet would we have you to carry in your two ships appointed for the *Molloccos*, such quantity of pintados, monies, and other provisions, as may suffice to lade the said two ships.

20 Leaving other things of the state of your business to consideration, and the state and health of men, etc.

Thus we have touched many particulars of our business. Notwithstanding, many other things may occur which may greatly concern us, which we must leave to your good considerations to deal therein, as time and occasion shall offer you occasion, commending unto your care the state of such as shall fall sick in the voyage, either outward or inward, that they may be comforted; and if they die, see that their goods may be kept in safety, and their wills and dispositions thereof so well testified, that there grow not the like suspicion of the truth of some of their wills, as hath been had of the wills of others that died in the last voyage.

And forasmuch as the days of man's life are limited, and the certain limitation thereof only known unto God, we do hereby ordain and provide, that, whereas we have appointed and placed you, the said *Henrie Middleton* in the Red Dragon, as general or governor of the whole fleet; and you, master *Christofer Colthurst*, as lieutenant-general and principal merchant, in the Hector; and you, master *Roger Style*, our principal merchant, in the Ascension; and you, master *William Keeleinge*, another of our principal merchants, in the Susan — if, therefore, it shall happen any of you to
21 Any dying, others to be placed as they were first appointed, and so consequently, etc.
decease in this voyage, we do ordain that he that in place and order by us appointed to go as principal in every ship, which shall survive the party deceased, shall and may, by the appointment of tbe general, *shall* [ship] himself in the ship out of which the said party did decease, and hold his place in the same ship, and the place that the party deceased held generally in the voyage; and so a succession to be held from the general to the lieutenant, from the lieutenant to the principal merchant placed in the Ascension, from the principal merchant of the Ascension to the principal merchant placed in the Susan. And if it shall happen all the principals of the several ships to decease (as God forbid), the like succession to hold and be kept by the several merchants appointed to hold the second places in every the said ships, and so in succession from one to another, according as the several merchants hold place in every ship.

22 Where master *Starkey* shall be shipped, if he return home.

Provided always, that if master *William Starkey*, our agent resident at *Bantam*, do come home in the return of the ships, then we do require you, our general and principal merchants, to take especial order that he be provided for and placed in such ship as he shall be shipped as a man that we hold to be had in good regard, and to be respected accordingly; and if any of the principal merchants' places fall void by the death of any of them, or otherwise, that then he supply that place in his return homewards.

23 Master *Colthurst*, lieutenant, to succeed master *Henrie Middleton*, general, if he decease, unto whom command of the

And lastly, whereas his majesty, under his great seal of *England*, hath appointed you, the said master *Henrie Middleton*, the general and principal governor of all his subjects employed in the voyage; and you, the said master *Christofer Colthurst*, to be lieutenant-general; and if you, the said *Christofer Colthurst*, survive the said *Henrie Middleton*, then to succeed him in the place of governor or general, without appointing any further succession, by like warrant to any that is employed in the said voyage; and that it lieth not in us to give to any of the residue of our principal merchants any warrant for the correction of offences by penal laws, to be executed upon the bodies of any his majesty's subjects, we do, in that behalf, as to men having reason and discretion, and to men that fear God, offer unto your considerations the benefit of order and peaceable government in matters and enterprises undertaken for a common good, reposing in you, our several merchants, and all you, our several officers, appointed and entertained in this voyage, a special hope, trust, and confidence that you will accord and agree together, and remain in friendship and amity, to do and execute your uttermost endeavours for the benefit of the voyage, without contention, discord, or emulation to be used amongst you, guiding yourselves therein by that general regiment and sea-government which our English fleets do use when they sort themselves together; having especial and due respect to him that is the principal or *cape* [sic] merchant. So we commend you and your endeavours to God's providence, who guide you with his fear, and defend you from all dangers. Amen.

men shall be as in the general.

24 Post scriptum.

As touching such factors as are to be left in the country, or of those which go now in these ships, we do agree and give order, by this our commission, that the appointment of the said factors to reside in those places shall be at the direction and consent of you our general, master *Christofer Colthurst*, master *Starkey*, and master *Morgan*, or any three of you, wherein we hope you will have that consideration as to make choice of the fittest. Neither let the placing of our factors in the several ships, as they are already placed, be any rule to you, or any ground for them to enjoy those places of employment wherein you are to bestow them, otherwise than they shall be found able and meet to deserve that trust of employment.

25 Unto whom the power of the factors placing shall be in, and our placing to be no rule.

26 What we were advised of out of the Low-Countries, from *Bantam*, since all things were in a readiness.

The ships being ready to depart, and all our commissions and instructions being resolved upon and finished, we received letters out of the Low-Countries, which came from our factors from the *East Indies*, by the Dutch ships, viz.: from master *William Starkey*, of the 22nd of June, and two other letters, one from *Edmond Scott*, and the other from *Thomas Tudd*, both dated the 17th of August 1603; by which latter letters we were advised of the death of master *Starkey* and master *Morgan*, and of others who were left at *Bantam;* and also of the damage that happened unto us, in our goods burnt by fire in the Dutch warehouse; together with the disappointment of our intended voyage to the *Molloccos*, by the contrariety of winds. All which things being considered, we take them, as they were indeed, the hand of God, who disposeth of all enterprises according to his good will and pleasure; which accidents, howsoever, by the death of our said principal factors, they do, in some manner, move us to alter our said commissions and advices, so far as we had appointed any thing to be done by the advice of the said master *Starkey* and master *Morgan;* yet in substance we purpose to hold our former resolutions for the following of our business, and, instead of the persons deceased, we wish you to advise and use conference with the factors remaining whom you find most apt and able to assist you in the direction of the business; and, touching your proceedings in the voyage from *Bantam* to the *Molloccos*, after order for lading of the Dragon and the Susan with pepper, to return for *England*, being taken, we think it fit you, captain *Middleton*, prepare yourself with all speed to go for *Banda*, and do furnish yourself with the most aptest and fittest of our factors to attend you, and to be left at *Banda* for the further following of that trade, according as it may be found likely to bring benefit to the Company; wherein you are, according to your good discretion and consideration, to use the more or fewer factors to be left there, as you shall find the more or less hope of benefit to be made by their residence in that place, not forgetting the Company's desire, as near as you can possibly, to clear the former voyage, according to our former direction, by a discreet and reasonable valuation of the remainder. And for the accomplishing of lading at *Banda* in the *Moloccos*, you, our said general, are to take with you so much of the commodities remaining in our factors' hands at *Bantam*, as they think will serve for the providing of your lading at the *Molloccos*, according to the proportion given by sir *James Lancaster* to provide, remembering that the Dutchmen bought of *Spillesbe* [captain Spilberg] the like commodities, to carry to the *Molloccos* for the better furnishing of their landing. But for your better assurance lest the said commodities should not be in request there, you shall do well to take with you 10,000, 15,000, or 20,000 royals-of-eight, as you shall think meet; and, being so furnished, both by wares and money, you may both provide you lading, and supply your factors which you shall think fit to leave to reside there with sufficient stock for provision of cloves and mace against another year. This project being laid down for the trade at *Banda*, you shall do well, in your going thither, to touch at the island of *Amboyna* [Amboina], or any other island by the way where cloves may be had, and to furnish yourself with what quantity you can get, whereby you may the less depend upon your provision of cloves at *Banda;* and having directed and ordered your business for the *Moloccos*, then, upon your return to *Bantam*, to take full and perfect knowledge of the whole state of our business, and to leave ten or twelve factors there with such stock as shall remain unemployed, or as may be spared, our ships being laden—admonishing the factors to be more careful to buy their pepper at the best advantage than they have been, and to buy of the largest pepper, which here beareth the best estimation; and unless you shall find it very necessary that some factors be left at *Banda*, we are of opinion, and do like well, that the residue of our factors be holden altogether at *Bantam;* but herein we leave you to your own experience, as you shall find the course most convenient. And so, as before, commend you to God's providence.

And whereas our factors deceased do appear to have left some effects behind them, which must have means to come to the hands of such as have interest therein, we do wish you to take order that all things that do appear to belong unto them be duly and truly inventoried, and shipped apart by themselves, and their wills safely kept and brought home, together with their books and notes of their buying and sellings, whereby their estates were increased and gotten; to the end that the Company may be satisfied that they have been well dealt withal therein, and their friends receive that which shall rightfully appertain unto them.

[No. IV.—A letter from James I. to the king of Bantam, sent by captain Henry Middleton. 1604.][1]

A l're from his matie to the kinge of Bantam in the East Indies, by sr Henrie Middleton.

James, by the grace of God kinge of England, Scotland, ffraunce, and Ireland, defendor of the faith, etc.: To the greate and mightie kinge of Bantam, and of the dominions and territories adioyning, greetinge. Whereas the right of inheritaunce and possession of theis or kingdomes of England, ffraunce, and Ireland, by the decease of or late deare sister of ffamous memory is discended vpon vs, and ioyned to or other principalities and kingdomes wch we form'lie enioyed, we being established and setled in the possession thereof, haue received into or hands vpon the retourne of sr James Lancaster and other of or subiects from yor maties kingdomes and territories wth their shipps and marchandize, not onelie yor princelie l'res directed and sent to or said deceased sister, but alsoe yor kinde present wch did accompanie the same, holding or selfe after her deaceased interressed there in by the right of or crowne and septer. Vpon the p'vsall of wch l'res we weare possessed wth noe small ioye, that yor matie had soe gratiouslie accepted the comeing of or subiects into yor dominions and kingdomes, and soe fauorablie and royallie delt wth them whilest they aboade and contynued theare in traffique wth yor subiects; of all wch ffavors and other yor maties princelie p'ceedings wth them or said subiects, sr James Lancaster hath made vnto vs verie lardge and ample relac'on. This introducc'on being made into a mutuall amitie and entercourse betweene yor matie and vs, we are desirous to nourrish and contynue the same by all good meanes and oportunities that may be thought vpon or conceiued on or p'te; and to that end we haue geven lycence to diurs of or subiects to prepare and sett forth a new voyadge towards yor countries and kingdomes, amongest wch manie of them wch were in the former voyadge are desirous for the good and honorable vsadge they formerlie founde by yor princelie favor, to visitt the same againe; others vpon their

[1 From the India-House Mss.—This document is printed literatim, but the punctuation has been revised.]

reporte are encouradged, not w^{th}standing the longe and daungerous nauigac'on, to see the state and manner of behavio^{r} of people in countries farr remote. Theis considerac'ons moueing both vs and o^{r} subiects to visitt yor ma^{ties} countries with lawfull and peaceable traffique of m'chandize, we doubt not but your ma^{tie} will be well pleased therew^{th}; and not onelie soe, but wth the continuance of an entercourse from yeare to yeare of o^{r} m'chaunts wth their shipps and goods into yor kingdomes, whome we dare be bold to com'end to yor ma^{tie} for a people civill and iust in their dealeing and trade, and euery way as able to furnish yor ma^{tie} and yor people wth all such comodities wch this parte of the world doth yeald, or affordeth, as any nac'on or people what soeu^{r} wch heretofore haue made trade or traffique wth yor people. And because a capitulac'on and establishing of amitie [and] entercourse to be contynued betweene yor ma^{tie} and vs cannot convenientlie be p'formed by discourse of l'res, o^{r} seu'all kingdomes being soe farr distant and remote th'one from the other, we therefore pray yor ma^{tie} to giue eare therein to this bearer, and to giue him creditt in whatsoeu^{r} he shall vndertake or promyse in o^{r} name concerninge the same, wch we promyse for o^{r} p'te in the worde of a prince shall be p'formed, and will be redie gratefullie to requite any loue, kindnes, or favo^{r} that o^{r} said subiects shall receiue at yor ma^{ties} hands. And in token of o^{r} princelie loue to yor ma^{tie}, we send you by this bearer a remembraunce and kindnes, wch we pray you to accept as from one that wisheth vnto yo^{u} all good successe and happines. And soe comend yor ma^{tie} to the tuic'on of the most highe God.

[No. V.—A LETTER FROM JAMES I. TO THE KING OF . . . . . , SENT BY CAPTAIN HENRY MIDDLETON. 1604.][1]

James, by the grace of God, *king* of England, ffraunce, and Ireland, defendor of the faith, etc. — To the greate and mightie kinge of . . . . . .

A l're to the kings of the East Indies.

WHEARAS Almightie God, in his infinite and vnsearchable wisedome and gratious providence, hath soe disposed of his blessings, and of the good things of this world, created and ordayned for th' use of man, that the same however they be brought forth, and doe either originallie growe and are gathered, or otherwyse composed and made, some in [one] countrie, and some in another, yet are they, by the industrie of man, directed by the hand of God, dispersed and sent out into all the partes of the world, that his wonderfull bountie in his creatures may appeare vnto all nac'ons, his Maiestie haueing soe ordaned, that noe one place should inioye, as the natiue comodities thereof, all things app'tayninge to mans vse, but that one countrie should haue need of another, and out of the aboundance of the ffruits wch some region enioyeth, the necessities or wants of another should be supplied, by wch meanes men of seu'all and ffar remote countries haue comerce and traffique, one wth another, and by their interchandge of comodities are linked to gether in amitie and frendshipp.

This consideration, most noble kinge, together wth the ho: [norable] reporte of yor matie for the well entertayninge of straungers that visitt yor country in loue and peace, wth lawfull traffique of marchandize, haue moued vs to giue licence to diuers [of] or subiects, who haue beene stirred vpp wth a desier by a longe and daungerous navigac'on to finde out and visitt yor territories and dominions,

[[1] From the India-House Mss.—I find it stated, in a note to the preceding article, that another letter was also "written from the kinge to some other prince in those p'ts, of the tenor of that form'lie from queene Elizabeth." It must have been the letter now produced, and which was intended to be addressed and delivered as circumstances might require. It is printed LITERATIM, but the punctuation has been revised.]

being famous in theis p'ts of the world for honorable m'chandizeing, and to offer you comerce and traffique, in buying, bartering, and enterchandgeing of comodities wth yor people, according to the course of m'chaunts; wch commerce and enterchandging, yf yor [majesty] shall accept of, and shall receiue and entertayne o^r^ marchaunts wth favo^r^, according to the hope that gaue them encouragm^t^ to attempt soe long and daungerous a voiadge, you shall finde them a people, in their dealing and conversac'on, of that justice and ciuillitie, that you shall not mislike of their repaire to yor dominions, and vpon furder conference and inquisic'on had wth them, both of the kinds of their m'chandize brought in their shipps, and of other necessarie com'odities wch o^r^ dominions may afford, yt may appeare to yor ma^tie^ that, by their meanes, you may be furnished, in their next retourne into yor ports, in better sorte then you haue beene heretofore supplied, either by the Spaniard or Portugall, who, of all other nac'ons in the parts of Europe, haue onelie hitherto frequented yor countrie wth trade of m'chandize, and haue been the onelie ympedim^ts^, both to o^r^ subiects, and diuers other marchaunts in the parts of Europe, that they haue not hitherto visited yor countrie wth trade, whilest the said Portugalls p'tended them selues to be the souereigne lords and princes of all yor territories, and gaue yt out that *the* [they] held yor nac'on and people as subiects to them, and, in their stiles and titles, doe write them selues kings of the East Indies.

And yf yor ma^tie^ shall, in yor princelie ffavo^r^, accept wth good likeing this first repaire of o^r^ m'chaunts vnto yor countries, resorting thither in peaceable traffique, and shall intertaine this their first voyadge, as an introducc'on to a furder continuance of league and frendshipp betweene yor ma^tie^ and vs, and of comerce and entercourse betweene yor subiects and ours, we haue geven order to this, o^r^ principall marchaunt, yf yor ma^tie^ should be pleased therew^th^, to leaue in yor countrie some such of o^r^ said marchaunts as he shall make choise of, to reside in yor dominions, vnder yor princelie and saffe p'tecc'on, vntill the retourne of another fleete, wch we shall send vnto you, who may, in the meane tyme, learne the languadge of yor countrie, and applie their behavier, as yt may best sorte, to converse wth yor ma^ties^ subiects, to th' end that amitie and freindshipp being intertayned and begunn, the same may the better be contynued, when o^r^ people shalbe instructed, how to direct them selues according to the ffashions of yor countrie.

And because, in the considerac'on of the entertayning of amytie and freindshipp, in the establishinge of enterco'se to be contynued betweene vs, there may be required, on yor maties behalfe, such promyse or capitulac'on to be p'formed by vs, wch we cannot, in theis or l'res, take knowledge of, we therefore pray yor matie to giue eare therein to this bearer, and to giue him creditt, in whatsoeu' he shall p'myse or vndertake in or name, concerning or amitie and entercourse, wch promyse, we for or p'ts, in the worde of a prince, will see p'formed, and will be redie gratefullie to requite any loue, kindnes, or fauor, that or subiects shall receiue at yor maties hands; praying yor matie, for or better satisfacc'on of yor kinde acceptaunce of this or loue and amitie offered yor highnes, you would, by this bearer, giue testimonie thereof, by yor princelie l'res, directed vnto vs, wch shall giue vs greate and wonderfull contente. And thus, etc.

[No. VI.—A letter from sir Thomas Smith, governor of the East-India Company, to captain William Keeling. 1604.][1]

A seuerall l're wth the bills and inuoyces to each shipp, from Grauesend.

Loueinge freind m^r Kealing, heereinclosed wee doe send you the bill of lading of the money and app'ell laden in that shipp the Suzan, together wth a generall invoice as well of all the money and goods in the 4 shipps, as alsoe of all that wch form'lie remaned in the countrie of the East Indies, to th'end both you and all the ffacto^rs there may take knowledge and see what theyhaue in chardge; for the better ordering and disposeing where of, both you and they are to follow such direcc'on as we haue alredie sufficientlie and att lardge geuen you in o^r l'res and comission, wherein we nothinge doubt of yor due care and considerac'on, eu'y one of you in his place, in dischardg of yor duties accordinge to that trust we doe repose in you. Thus wishing you a faire winde to be bound, we comend vs vnto you, and comitt you and all yor companie to the most safe p'tecc'on of the Highest, whoe send you a safe and speedie passadge to yor desired porte, and graunte vs a happie meetinge to Gods glorie and to o^r comforts, etc. In Grauesend, the 25th of March 1604. Signed by s^r Thomas Smyth.

[[1] From the India-House Mss.—The general invoice which accompanied this farewell letter is a desideratum. The amount of cash exported, and the particulars of the merchandise which remained at Bantam, are stated in No. III. This document is printed LITERATIM, but the punctuation has been revised.]

[No. VII.—A remembrance by captain Henry Middleton, for the factors left at Bantam. 1605.][1]

A remembrance for *Gabriell Towerson*, *Robert Browne*, *George Woodnoth*, *Henrie Sydall*, and *John Saires*, the first of October 1605, in *Bantam*.

Sir *Henrie Middleton's* remembrances left at *Bantam*, and the names and wages of those there.

The first thing you are to have care of after the departing of the ships is to get workmen to oversee all the decayed places of your warehouses, and to see them sufficiently repaired, and to remove all the carriages with such lumber of timber as lieth scattered about the yard into some warehouse, to avoid the danger of fire, otherwise it is very doubtful all, both house and goods, will be lost; and, in any case, let not at any time anything apt to take fire lie near the warehouse-doors, that thereby you be not debarred to succour it, if need shall require.

Also, I think it fit you sell such *Java* goods as are likely of perishing for pepper, if you think you can make sale thereof to the Company's profit, either to the *Hollenders*, or *China* junks when they shall come hither; and not to bestow the charge of cleansing it, but to sell it as it cometh to your hands. If not, to sell for royals and such monies as you shall make thereof, to be put out to the Company's profit, as in your good discretion you shall think most meet. And for those goods brought back by me from the *Molloccos*, with some other in the warehouse, which will better sell there than here, as master *Browne* and master *Woodnoth* can best inform you, I would not that any of them should be sold there, but be carefully looked unto, that they perish not for lack of caring; and if the Hector and Susan should return again, as I make small doubt by God's help but they will, you may do as you

[[1] From the India-House Mss.—This document, with regard to proper names and general orthography, is printed on the same plan as the third article of the present appendix.]

and them that come in them shall think most meet; but my opinion is, the greater ship is fittest to take in the goods and proceed for the *Molloccos*—for that, I doubt not, there will be *Molloccos* goods enough in your warehouse to lade her with cloves. You are to have great care you make no debts but such as you may at all times, after the expectation of our ships, which will be about eighteen months hence, have in at two or three months' warning: the reason is, I am persuaded they will bring such order from the Company to clear all matters out of the countrie, wherein they bear so great a venture, without profit, and therefore about that time you may have made sale of all the *Java* wares in the house, to be employed in pepper or any other commodity which you think may rebound to the Company's most profit.

And whereas, master *Gabriell Towerson,* I am possessed with a conceit of your discretion and good government, I have made choice of you to be commander over all this place; but to take the counsel and advice of master *Browne,* master *Woodnoth,* master *Sydall,* and master *Saires* in all matters, that the Company may be the better assured of all things that passeth.

And if it please God to lay his hand upon you, master *Towerson,* and take you out of this world, I would have you to give over your place to master *Browne;* and if you, *Robert Browne,* should die, then to master *Woodnoth;* and if you, *George Woodnoth,* shall die, then it shall rest in your discretion to make your choice of master *Sydall* and master *Sayrs,* which of they two you think fittest for such a place, always having a care to leave your business in the best and plainest manner you can: also I do appoint you, master *Browne,* to be bookkeeper for all matters in this place.

And for so much as the last voyage there was no order prescribed by the general, to such merchants as he left there, for the keeping of each one his particular estate in writing, so that thereby they seemed to neglect the same, as by proof we find—for not any of the deceased have left any writing concerning their own estates behind them—therefore I do ordain that every merchant left here by me do keep an account of his own business, for the better satisfying of the Company, and his friends to whom he shall bequeath his goods, if it please God to call him out of this life.

You are to be very careful for the overlooking of all your goods, and so that you suffer them not lie near the ground; for if they do, it will both rot them, and breed worms in them, as by experience we have found; and look that once a month all the goods be carried out to airing, and in so doing, I hope nothing will come to loss.

You are also to use good husbandry in charges of housekeeping, for that the Company are at great charge to maintain so many men upon so small a stock; and what provision is bought for the house, my will is, that there be no partiality therein, but let all the merchants' fare be alike, and not some to have command and the rest be without.

My desire is that you endeavour yourselves to hold friendship with the *Hollenders,* and suffer no evil speeches to pass by them by any of our people; and although the meaner sort of them be rude, I find that their commanders be desirous to live in amity and love with us. Therefore, if you hear any matter pretending at any time against them by the people of the country, that you advertise them thereof, for they have promised on their behalf to do the like; for if the people of the country perceive we be linked in one, they will be advised how they attempt anything against any of our nations—therefore you must be careful there be no occasions offered on our behalf. And look what order our late general, sir *James Lancaster,* left for the payment of mens' wages here in this place; I do hold it most fit the same order be observed still, only you are to pay no wages to *Lawrence* the surgeon and *Edward Ellimore,* who be not their own men, but servants, and therefore they must at all times be *soe plied* [supplied] by you of all such things as they shall necessary want, and the rest of the wages to be reserved to the use of their masters whom they serve.

If there be any of the meaner sort of men, I mean save the merchants, that shall misbehave themselves towards you, master *Towerson,* or any of the merchants or otherwise, it shall rest in your discretion to punish them, whereby they may reform themselves; and as for the merchants, I leave them with you, I know their discretion to be such that I dare undertake they will give no occasion of offence.

Thus, desiring you all to live in unity and love together, and to bear one with another, and not to take everything at the worst that shall be spoken, and that you meet all together at morning and at evening prayer; and so doing God will bless and prosper all you take in hand: and so I take my leave of you, praying God to save, bless, and defend you all. Amen.

The names of the men, with their wages left by me, *Henrie Middleton*, at *Bantam*, beginning their pay the first day of October 1605.

	li.	s.	d.
Master *Gabriell Towerson*, 6*li.* per month . .	06	00	00
Master *Robert Browne*, 6*li.* per month . .	06	00	00
George Woodnoth, 3*li.* 6*s.* 8*d.* per month . .	03	06	08
John Sayers, 3*li.* 6*s.* 8*d.* per month . . .	03	06	08
Henrie Sydall, 3*li.* 6*s.* 8*d.* per month . . .	03	06	08
Richard Cotton, 1*li.* 5*s.* 00*d.* per month . .	01	05	00
Lawrence Sturdynan, 23*s.* per month . . .	01	03	00
Richard Claxon, 24*s.* per month . . .	01	04	00
John Delane, 22*s.* per month	01	02	00
John Bemunde, 26*s.* per month . . .	01	06	00
Edward Preston, 20*s.* per month . . .	01	00	00
Edward Collenes, 22*s.* per month . . .	01	02	00
John Smyth, 22*s.* per month	01	02	00
Matthew Price, 24*s.* per month . . .	01	04	00
James More, 24*s.* per month	01	04	00
Michaell Marlin, 26*s.* per month . . .	01	06	00
Edward Elsmore, 28*s.* per month . . .	01	08	00
Austen Spaulden, 26*s.* per month . . .	01	06	00
[sic]	37½	02	

[No. VIII.—A letter from James I. in reply to the king of Ternatè. 1607.][1]

His matie to the kinge of the Molloccos.

His matie to the kinge of the Molloccos.

James, by the grace of God kinge of Greate Brittaine, ffraunce, and Ireland, defendor of the faith, etc. To the mightie kinge of the Molloccos and of the teritories and dominions adioyneing. Att the retourne of or subiects from their last voyadge in yor countries, we receiued from you a l're of greate kindnes, and a bahar of cloues, wch we tooke very kindlie as a testimony of your desire to enterteyne amitie wth vs, but especiallie wee weare pleased to vnderstand of yor kindnes towards them in matters conc'ning their trade and traffique wth you, wch hath incouraged them to p'ceede in yt, and vs to recomend them to you and yor p'tecc'on agaynst any that would oppose agaynst them or molest them in their trads, in as ample manner as we would be willing to doe to any of yors, yf their desire shall be to visitt or countries. And whereas we vnderstand that some Hollenders whoe traffique wth you doe oppose them selues agaynst or subiects wth euill speeches and other practizes to hinder their trade, although we doubt not but yt in yor owne judgement you can easilie conceiue that m'chaunts, not onelie of diuers nac'ons, but of one and the same nation, will ofte tymes calumniate each others for diuers respects, and hinder what they cann those that happen into the saime trade wch *the* [they] vse; yet haue we thought good to assure you soe much by or l're, that their superiors and gou'nors will disallowe them in that practise, being wth vs in verie

[1 From the India-House Mss.—This letter was written in reply to the letter of the king of Ternatè which accompanies the text. He is styled king of *the Molloccos* by way of compliment. The document is printed literatim, but the punctuation has been revised.]

good amitie. Wherefore we doubt not but you will graunte vnto o[r] subiects ffreedome of quiet traffique wth you, wth saffetie for their p'sons, ships, and goods, and libertie to establish a ffactorie theare, yf they shall desire yt, according to yo[r] princelie offer in yo[r] said l're. And in the meane tyme, for a token of o[r] good will and desire to enterteyne yo[r] princelie amitie, we haue by this bearer o[r] servant sent you a small present, wch we pray you to accept. Where wth we comend yor ma[tie] to the tuition of the most high God. Dated att o[r] pallace of Westminster the 23th of ffebruarie 1606 [1607].

[No. IX.—A LETTER FROM JAMES I. IN REPLY TO THE KING OF TIDORÈ. 1607.][1]

From his ma^{tie} to the kinge of Tedore.

His matie to the kinge of Tedore.

RIGHT high, etc. Att the retourne of o^{r} m'chaunts from their voyadge into yor countries, we receiued a token from you wch we tooke very kindelie; and vnderstanding by their reporte that they had found good vsadge of you and yor subiects in their trade, and they being incourraged thereby to retourne agayne, we thought yt ffitt to lett you p'ceaue by o^{r} l'res what good reporte they haue made of yor freindlines towardes them, and to praye the continuance thereof, soe as they may continue their traffique wth yor ffavo^{r}, and wth saffetie of their p'sons, ships, and goods, in such manner as we will doe to any of yo^{rs} that haue desire to visitt theis p'ts; and yf in any thinge we may doe you kindnes, you shall be assured of yt. In the meane tyme we haue sent you by this bearer, o^{r} servant, a token of o^{r} good will, wch we desire may eu^{r} increase betweene you and vs. Dated att o^{r} pallace of Westminster the 23th of ffebruarie 1606 [1607].

[1 From the India-House MSS.—This letter was written in reply to the letter of the king of Tidorè which accompanies the text. The document is printed LITERATIM, but the punctuation has been revised.]

[No. X.—A letter from James I. in reply to the king of Bantam. 1607.][1]

His highnes to the kinge of Java Maior.

Right high, etc. Att the retourne of o^r^ subiects from their last voyadge into yor countries, we rec^d^ from you both a l're of great kindnes and twoe bezar stones, both wch we tooke verie kindlie, as a testimony of yor [desire] to enterteyne amitie wth vs; especiallie we were pleased [to un]derstand by their reporte how kindlie they were vsed in yor cou[ntrie] in matters concerning their traffique, wch hath incouraged th[em] to p'ceede in yt, and vs to recomend them to you and yor p'tecc'on, agaynst any that would oppose agaynst them or molest them in their said trad^s^, in as ample manner as we would be willinge to doe to any of yo^rs^ yf their desires shall be to visitt o^r^ countries.

His highnes to the kinge of Jaua Maior.

To testifie vnto you o^r^ kinde acceptaunce of yor favo^r^ shewed them, and o^r^ desire to continue amitie wth you, we haue sent by this bearer, o^r^ servant, a token of o^r^ loue, wch we hope shall alwaies continue and encrease betweene vs. Dated att o^r^ pallace of Westmin' the 23th of ffebruarie 1606 [1607].

[[1] From the India-House Mss.—This letter was written in reply to the letter of the king of Bantam which accompanies the text—the address, as in the reply to the king of Ternatè, being a piece of state-flattery. The portions within brackets are supplied by conjecture: the rest is printed LITERATIM. James I. was often styled *his highness*, as may be seen in the *Annales* of Stow.]

[No. XI.—A LETTER FROM JAMES I. TO THE SABANDAR OF NERA. 1607.][1]

From his ma^{tie} to Nere.

His ma^{tie} to ye sabander of Nere.

ATT the retourne of o^{r} m'chaunts from their trade in that countrie we receiued from you a bahar of nutmeggs for a token of o^{r} good will, wch we accepted wth all kindnes. And we vnderstoode by them howe freindlie they had beene intertayned by you in their traffique, wch hath incourraged them to attempt it agayne, and vs to recomend them vnto yor ffavo^{r} and p'tecc'on, soe as they may be suffered quietlie to continue their said trad^{s} wth saffetie and good vsadge of their p'sons, shipps, and goods; and we shall be redie to requite yt wth any kindnes to yo^{u} or yo^{rs}; and in the meane tyme haue sent you by this bearer, o^{r} servant, a token of o^{r} good will, wch we desire may eu^{r} increase betweene you and vs. ffrom o^{r} pallace at Westminster the 23th of ffebr. 1606 [1607].

[No. XII.—A LETTER FROM JAMES I. TO THE SABANDAR OF LANTORE. 1607.]

From his ma^{tie} to Luntor.

From his ma^{tie} to the sabander of Luntor.

ATT the retourne of o^{r} m'chaunts from their trade in that countrie we vnderstande by them how freindlie they had beene interteyned by yo^{u} in their traffique, wch hath incourraged them to attempt yt agayne, and vs to recomend them to yor ffavo^{r} and p'tecc'on, soe as they may be suffered quietlie to continue their said trades wth saffetie and good vsadge of their p'sons, shipps, and goods; and we shall be redie to requite yt wth any kindnes to you or yo^{rs}; and in the meane tyme haue sent you by this bearer, o^{r} servant, a token of o^{r} good will, wch we desire may euer encrease betweene you and vs. Dated att o^{r} pallace of Westmin' the 23th of ffebruarie 1606 [1607].

[1 From the India-House Mss.—These two letters refer to the proceedings of captain Colthurst at Banda, in 1605; and are printed LITERATIM.]

[No. XIII.—A LETTER FROM MASTER GABRIEL TOWERSON, CHIEF FACTOR AT BANTAM, TO HIS BROTHER. 1607.][1]

Laus Deo, this 30th of Aprill 1607, in Bantam.

BROTHER TOWERSON, my last vnto you of the 26th of October 1606, p' the West Fresland, wherein I wrote vnto you as then the tyme serued; since wch tyme here hath not happened anie matter worthy the wryting of concerning my owne busines, wch is in so good a forwardnes, that I thingke the tyme verie long that our shippes were come to make an end of this yrksome living in this place, yf it shall please the Almightie.

The principall newes in these parts proceedeth from the Hollanders busines, ffor they are the men that beare the greatest swaye, whose reports, for want of other matter, I will advertise you of.

At this present here is an admirall, Cornelius Mataliphe the youngr, who dep'ted out of Holland in Maye 1605, having a fleete of XI shippes,[2] keeping on their course vntill the 24th of Iune, when they fell wth the iland Maio, where they watered and tarried 14 daies. The 9 of Iulie they sett saile from thence, keeping on their course vntill the 28th of August, when they came to anchor at the iland of Annabo, where they accorded wth the people of the place to refresh and water, wch is a verie fitt place for that purpose; there is good refreshing of orringes and divers other fruits. This iland lieth in two degrees southerly of the line; it is a verie pleasant land, the people are of color blacke, and goe all naked, saue a small peece of lynnen to hide their privities. The 5 of September they sett saile from Annabo, and on the 28 of October they were thwart the Cape Bona Speransa. The 9 of

[1 From the State-paper Office. East-India papers.—This document seems to be in the handwriting of Towerson, and is printed LITERATIM.]

[2 Admiral Matelief sailed from the Texel on the twelfth of May 1605, N.S. The burden of the eleven ships amounted to 5820 tons, and the number of men was 1440. An ample account of this voyage is contained in the *Recueil des voiages* edited by C. de Renneville.]

November they were troubled wth a great storme west-noth-west, in wch storme 6 of the fleete were seperated from the rest, wch the next daie mett agayne. The 21 of December they had sight of the iland Cerna, by the Hollanders called Moritius. The next daie they came to an ancho^{r}, where they found 2 Holland shippes, wch was Verhagen' shippe and the Great Horne, bound for Holland to this place: they had not lost a man, but one wch was killed abord the admirall by another of the same shippe. This iland of Moritius the Hollanders make greate recconing of: yt affoordeth good refreshing of fish, foules, and seales, wch are so tame that they take them at pleasure. The Hollanders doe contynually carrie thither goats and hoggs, and leaue them there to increase. At this iland they sett vpp their pinnaces. On the 18th of Ianuary they dep'ted from thence, being the nomber of 15 shippes and pynnaces. The 16 of March they came to the ilands of Nicobar; the 18, they fynding the wynde contrary, they came to an anchor, where the people of the countrie brought them fruits to exchaunge for other trifles.

Here at this place he did make the fleete acquaynted wth his pretence that he determyned to goe directly for Mallaca, and promised verie large offers to the company, if they tooke it either by force or otherwaies; the bay where they did ride, the admirall did newe name it by his owne name, Mataliphe. The 24 they sett saile from this baye of Mataliphe, and being entred into the straits they had sight of 2 ilands, to name, Pula Porro and Pula Pinassa. The 6 of Aprill 1606 they had sight of the maine of Mallaca, wth 2 ilands bearing east and west the one from the other. The 19 ditto they came in sight of the towne of Mallaca, and came to ancho^{r} wthin a league and $\frac{1}{2}$ of the said towne. Presently they manned there botes to fetch the shippes out of the rode, wch were 4 in nomber, wch the enemie p'ceaving, layd a trayne of powder in the one wch was newly come in, and forsooke her, and as the Hollanders did enter, she blewe vpp, where they lost 8 or 9 men: the other 3 being emptie, the Hollanders put fire to them, soe they burnt. The next daie the fleete wayed, and came nere the towne, where they did ancho^{r} in 5 or 6 fatham water, and shott of all their ordn'nce against the towne and castell, the enemie shooting but little at them. This night the admirall pretending to land his forces, but altering his mynde he purposed to staie the coming of the king of Iore, to whome he had sent a pynnace from the fleete, wth the Iore ambassadour wch they brought out of Holland. The 21 of Aprill they beganne to make a battrie from a small iland on the south side of the towne, where they planted 2 peeces of ordenaunce, and in the afternoone playd wth them against the towne; but from that daie to the 2 of Maie they shott no more, being to so small a purpose, but laye still, preventing the enimies pretenses and keeping watch that there should goe no succkers to the enimye: in w'che tyme they tooke many espialls, wch were sent out dailie to seeke to fire their shippes, of wch they tooke a boate wth 4 men, wch did confesse they were sent out for the same purpose by the governo^{r} of the towne. In this tyme there were 4 iunckes of Shumatra, wch came to helpe the Hollanders. The 7 ditto came the king of Iore to the fleete, but not so strong as was exspected.

The next daie in the afternoone, at high water, they landed all their forces on the west side of the towne, being of Hollanders and blakes 13 or 1400 men. At their first landing they were encountered by wth 3 or 4 companies of Portingales, but they retyred ymediatly to the fore towne, from whence they did skirmish wth their musketts. But the Hollanders bending a peece of orden'nce against them after an hower skermish, the enemie did forsake the fore towne, setting yt a fire, and fled into the strong towne. The next daie, being the 9 ditto, the Hollander tooke in the fore towne, where they made their first battarie vpon the maine. The admirall being tould of the armado, sent aborde most of his men and orden'nce agayne, leaving a shore sufficient to keepe that wch they had begunne; and so yt contynued for the space of 14 daies. The 24 they did begynne to beleager the towne round about, making and fortifying themselues in quarters, where they planted feild peeces so farre as the east side, wch they did w'thout any resistaunce of the enemye. There were divers slaues wch did daily come out of the towne, wch complayned greatly of hunger.

The admirall having caused his men a shore agayne, and leaving his shippes so weakely manned, did bethinke himself of the armado coming vpon him, sent a shippe and pinnace to Cape Rochadoe to keepe watch there. In this tyme came into the fleete 2 Portingale shippes and 2 or 3 iunckes laded wth m'chaundizes, wch they made prize of. Vpon the 22 of Iune they built a skonce vpon the east strand, wch kept them in the towne in that sort that they could not goe out by land nor sea. The 10 of Iuly the Hollanders admirall sent a letter to the walls of the towne wth drumme and trumpett, in effecte to demaund the towne; but the Portingale wth vpbraving speeches willed the messenger to begonne, or he would send him wth shott from the walls. The next daie they beganne to shoote at the towne, w[ch] contynued that forenoone. The 14 ditto came 2 Holland shippes into the fleete, w[ch] had all this tyme bene missing. The 4 of August the shippes that kepte the watche brought newes that the armado was coming on. That night they gott most of the munic'on and orden'nce aborde. It was thought by the Hollanders, that yf the viceroye had kept on his course and followed the watch, they mought haue taken their shippes and murdered those a shore at ease. By the next night the Hollanders had gotten all the men and orden'nce aborde, when for a farwell, the Portingale did sallie out vpon them; but the Hollanders encountered them, and killed about 50[tie]; and the rest retiered agayne to the towne, and the Hollanders went quietly to their shippes, the admirall being the last man ashore himself. The 6 ditto they sett saile to meete wth the armado, w[ch] was 14 great shippes, 4 great gallies, and small frigotts, to the nomber in all 26, and by 3 a clocke in the afternoone they mett, where beganne the first fight: the viceroye shott the first shoote. This fight contynued verie hott on both p'ts for space of 2 howers, when the Portingales first bare vpp and came to anchor[r]; the Hollanders getting the winde of them, came to anchor[r] hard by them. The next morning they both wayed. The 2 of the Portingall shippes did borde the Phœnix, and sought to fire her, w[ch] tooke effecte; so she burnt downe to the water: the men were all saued.

Then beganne they to fight. The Portingales being full of men, sought to borde the other, and came wth 5 shippes at once to borde the vice-admirall; but finding her sides so hott, they were forced to keepe further off. 3 other sought to borde the admirall, w[ch] the shippe Middleborowe p'ceaving came to helpe, the w[ch] 5 shippes being thus to geather, fought for the space of 2 howers, vntill the Mauritious came vpp to helpe his admirall; and he shott a fire arrowe out of a crosbowe into the admirall of the Portingale, w[ch] tooke in that sort, that it burned 2 Portingale shippes and the shippe Middleborowe. So this daie were burnt 2 Holland shippes and 2 Portingall shippes downe to the water. The admirall and the third shippe being fast, so that to free them from burning came to composic'on that the Portingales should haue their liues saved, and should come to anchoʳ by the Hollanders admirall, wᶜʰ came to anchoʳ; but the Portingales shippe verie wisely was lett driue wᵗʰ the currant: the rest of the fleete thinking they had accorded wᵗʰ their admirall, lett her passe by them, wᶜʰ p'esently had helpe from their owne fleete, and toed in by the gallies. This fight lasted 6 or 7 howers, when both fleetes came to anchoʳ a league a sonder, and rested for that night. The 10 ditto both the fleets waied and fought 4 howers, but the Portingales gaue waie, so they came agayne to anchoʳ. The next daie the Hollanders having the winde of the enemies, the Portingales did waye likewise and shott verie fiercely for space of 4 or 5 howers, when the Portingales gaue waie, wᶜʰ the Hollanders followed a little, but the tide being spent they came to anchoʳ agayne. Att wᶜʰ tyme the Hollanders having want of powder and shott, lefte the armado, and went to Ior, to supplie the want; where they anchored the 5 of September, and remayned till the 22 ditto. On the 6 of October they determined to goe before Malaca againe to fight wᵗʰ the shippes. The 9 ditto they came in sight of the towne, where they see the shippes 7 in nomber, but the winde being contrarie they could not come at them vntill the 12 ditto. Then the admirall devyded his fleete into 3 squadrons: his owne shippe, the Great-Son, and the Provinses, was to giue the first assault, and went in among them, and brought one awaie wᵗʰ them; wᶜʰ the rest of the armado p'ceauing, sett saile to rescue, and did recouer her agayne, and brought her in wᵗʰ helpe of the gallies. Then came two of the armado to the vice-admirall, laying her aborde on both sides. But the vice-admirall plying his ordenaunce in that hott mann', that the one fell from him not able to helpe herself, the other fought so long till with shooting she tooke fire; att wᶜʰ tyme the vice-admirall was forced to lett loose, having staied so long that part of his gallarie was a fire.

Iust at that tyme, when they made accompte to haue entered, the Moritius laid the vice-admirall aborde and tooke her by composic'on, so they all came to anchoʳ agayne; the 13 ditto, they see the shippe that the vice-admirall the daie before fought wᵗʰ, driue, and tooke her wᵗʰout fighting; the same daie they tooke another shippe bound for Mallaca laden wᵗʰ m'chandize. This daie they did vnlade such shippes as they had taken, and burned the shippes before the towne. The 20 ditto they waied, and went to looke out for the rest of the fleete to destroye them, wch the Portingales p'ceauing, did, [burn] 3 of them, wch the daie before they had halled ashore, and tooke out their ordenaunce, mynding to saue them. By this tyme they had destroyed 8 of their best shippes. The 26 ditto, they dispeeded a small shippe, wch they had taken, for Ambon, laden wth cloth, having soldiers and others for the releife of that place. This shippe, after the fleete lefte her, was caste awaie, but the men and goods were saued; wch after bought 2 iunckes at Ior, and came here to Bantam the 13 of December. By these men had wee the first newes of this fleete. November the 5 they put to sea againe, and had sight of another shippe, wch they w'thout resistaunce tooke: yt was a shippe of St. Tome, of 400 tonnes. This shippe was taken before on the 2 of October, at Nicobars, by the Holland shippe wch was sent to trade vpon the coast of Corramandell. In this shippe was don Lewes de Loberto, wch was appointed admirall of the armadoe; and having cast awaie his shippe at Cape Comera, tooke passage in this m'chaunts shippe for Mallaca, and was taken againe, and is kept here in Bantam for a ransome of 6,000^c Rs.^o8. The 21 they had sight of 7 shippes more of the enemyes vnder an iland, but the winde was contrary that they could not come to them, but doing their best; wch the Portingale p'ceyuing, got them betwene 2 ilands a league a sonder, getting close aborde the shore, and brought all their ordenaunce to one side. The 28 ditto, the Hollanders came in among them, and did ancho^r w'thin saker shott of them. They sought manie waies to fire them, but the Portingale did still p'vent, by toing of the fires wth their frigotts and botes. The Hollanders seing yt would take no effecte, they dep'ted, keeping to and againe ther abouts to see if they would put to sea. The 26 of December, the admirall having taken order for the sending shippes to their lading ports, the vice-admirall wth 2 more to goe for Achene, from whence the Great-Son went for the cost of Corramandell; the admirall wth the rest, being 6 saile, arrived here in Bantam rode the 20 of Ianuary; and the 28 dep'ted from hence to the Moloces, to see if he could recover that place from the Spaniards. March the 14 the vice-admirall came into this rode wth the White Lyon. The admirall hath done manie good peeces of service in these parts, in securing

Achene, Ior, and Bantam, wch the Portingale did threaten to over runne with his great forces, and turne both the Hollanders and the English out from hence; wch vndoubtedly he had done, had it not pleased God to make this meanes to prevent him. But for Mallaca he hath given them so faire a warning that they will never be so neare getting it as they were; and surely had had it, if the armadoe had not come vppon them as he did. In all this tyme the Hollander loste vpward of 600 men, 2 great shippes, and 150^{c} Rs.^{o}8.

This p'esent 30 of Aprill 1607, here did arriue a pinnace from the Mauritious, or Cernne, wch brought newes, that the West-ffreesland, wch departed the 26 of October last from hence, is cast awaie vpon the Sand Iland, having saued all their men, but little of their goods, only the m'chaunts chests and a fewe fardells of mace. Thus desiring yo^{u} to comend me to all my freinds, I comitt yo^{u} to the protection of the Almightie, whome I beseech blesse and preserve yo^{u} and yo^{rs} to his good will and pleasure.

Yo^{r} loving brother,

GABRIELL TOWERSON.

[No. XIV.—A grant of license to sir Edward Michelborne to trade with Cathaia, China, etc. 1604.][1]

Octaba pars Pateñ **de anno RR** Jacobi **Secundo.**

Ð Liceñ spiał ꝑ Edwardo Michelborne Milite.

James by the grace of God etc. To all to whome these p'esents shall come sendeth greeting. Knowe yee that wee of our especiall grace ce'ten knowledg and meere moc'on for us our heires and successors have given and graunted and by these p'esents doe give and graunte to our trustie and welbeloved subject and se'vant sir Edward Michelborne knight one of our gentlemen pencioners and to his associats and companye with necessarie shippes and shipping free lib'tie and lycence to discover the countries and domynions of Cathaia, China, Japan, Corea, and Cambaia and the islands and countries thereunto adjoyning, and to marchandize and trade with the said seve'all countries and people inhabiting the said places not as yet frequented and traded unto by anie of our subjects or people without inte'rupc'on or hinderaunce of any whomsoever any restraint graunt or charter whatsoever to the contrarie hereof heretofore had graunted or made in any wise notw'thstanding In witnes whereof etc. T. R. apud Westm' vicesimo quinto die Junij etc.

P' bre' de privato sigillo etc.

This is a true and authentic copy from the original record remaining in the Chapel of the Rolls having been examined.

Thomas Palmer,
Ass^t. Record Keeper.
20 March 1851.

[[1] From the Chapel of the Rolls.—An account of the voyage made in pursuance of this license is printed in *Pvrchas his pilgrimes.*]

[No. XV.—A PROCLAMATION OF JAMES I. PROHIBITING THE IMPORTATION OF PEPPER EXCEPT BY THE EAST-INDIA COMPANY. 1609.][1]

BY THE KING.

¶ A proclamation inhibiting the importation of pepper from forraine parts, by any other persons then those of the East-Indian Company.

FORASMUCH as it is not vnknowen, that in former times when all or the greatest part of pepper, and other spices of the grouth of the East Indies, was brought into this our realme of England and principalitie of Wales by strangers onely, the same was then sold at very high rates, vntill such time as some of our owne merchants did themselues trade into those parts, and bringing in good quantities of those commodities, did sell the same at much lower prices, to the great reliefe and benefit of all our subiects in generall: And forasmuch as we doe finde, that the establishment and continuance of this trade, hath and will be more and more an occasion to imploy and encrease the great shipping of this kingdome, which hath heretofore bene out of vse, as being not so necessary for trade in countreys that are not so farre remote: For these, and some other reasons which haue bene deliuered vnto vs, being desirous to encourage this company, and to maintaine that trade by all good and lawfull meanes; And experience teaching vs, that if there should be, till the trade were better setled, a free and generall libertie for all persons whatsoeuer to bring in those commodities, it would be an occasion to ouerlay the trade, and strangers would of purpose vent their spices at small rates, thereby to enforce our owne subiects to desist from trading into those countreis: WE with the aduise of our priuie councell, haue thought fit, for some time to restraine the importation of pepper from forraine parts, by

[[1] From the State-paper Office. A printed copy.—It was reprinted in *A booke of proclamations*, London 1610. Folio.]

any others then by the merchants ioyntly of the East Indian Company. And therefore wee doe hereby will and commaund all person and persons whatsoeuer, either our naturall borne subiects, denizens, or strangers (not being the company aforesaid) to forbeare to bring into these our dominions of England and Wales, any pepper, directly or indirectly, vpon paine of forfeiture of the goods, and what other punishment they may incurre by any contempt and default herein. And to the end, this our pleasure may be more duely obserued, wee doe likewise charge and command all customers, comptrollers, searchers, waiters, farmours of our customes and their deputies, and all other our officers of the ports, within our territories aforesaid, that they doe not giue any bills of entrie for pepper that is brought in from forraine countreis, by any other then those who shall be knowen to bee of the company aforesaid: neither shall they suffer it to bee landed, or being so, shall seize the same to our vse as iustly forfaited. And moreouer, they and euery of them, shall vse their best meanes and endeuours to hinder and preuent all secret and fraudulent practizes of such as shall seeke to bring *it* [in] that commoditie, notwithstanding this our pleasure published to the contrary.

And because we are careful to preuent al inconueniences to the generality of our subiects, in case they should be hardly dealt with vnder this restraint, by those that haue the whole masse of pepper in their owne hands; although wee hold the company to be compounded of many good and honest merchants and others, yet because there is no societie wherein all are of one temper, and out of the care we haue alwayes had for the common good of all our people more then of any particuler societie; wee thought it not safe to repose so much confidence in a part of our people, as to leaue the whole body subiect to their wills, in matter of this nature.

And therefore hauing well examined what might be an indifferent price to yeeld to the merchants competent gaine for the maintenance of so great and long a trade, and so needfull for the support of nauigation, and yet not be ouerchargeable to the rest of our people, who haue on the other side dayly vse of that kinde of spice; wee haue conditioned with them, and limitted, that they shall vtter pepper at the rate of two shillings sixe pence the pound, and not exceed, to any that shall come or send for it, vpon paine of our high displeasure.

Which prouision, and limitation being made by vs in fauour of the communitie of our subiects, we haue thought good to publish and make knowen to all men, to the end that if it fall out, that such as by way of retaile doe vtter to our people dwelling in places remote from our citie of London, and other parts where shipping doeth ariue, that kinde of spice, there bee exacted any prices excessiue, it may appeare that the same is not for want of due prouision made to preuent it, but by the ouergreedinesse of those which shall sell it. In which consideration, although wee know, that there are many reasons, why those that sell by retaile, should demaund a further price then they pay for it here, as well in respect of the distance of place, forbearing of their money, as many other things incident to that kinde of trade : yet the better to containe them within the bounds of reasonable gaine, we haue thought good to make knowen thus much, thereby to expresse our owne care of our louing subiects, and to shew them the meanes whereby they may auoyd such further burden, as may bee cast vpon them by any that shall goe about by any vndue practise, to raise immoderate gaine, vnder colour or pretext of that course which we haue taken for the reasons aforesaid.

Giuen at Newmarket the last day of Nouember, in the seventh yeere of our reigne of Great Britaine, France and Jreland.

GOD SAUE THE KING.

¶ IMPRINTED AT LONDON by Robert Barker, printer to the kings most excellent maiestie.
ANNO 1609.

[No. XVI.—Extracts from Ludovico de Varthema and others on the Maluco Islands.]

(1)

"Ca. della insula Monoch doue nascono li garoffoli.

Smonta'mo in questa insula Monoch, la q'le e molto piu piccola che no' e Bandan, ma la gente si e pegiore che quilli de Ba'dan, & uiueno pure a quel modr [modo], & so'no un pocho piu bianchi & lo aere e un poco piu ferddo [freddo]. Qui nascono li garoffoli, & in molte altre insule circu'uicine, ma so'no piccole & deshabitate. Lo arbore delli garoffoli si e p'prio co'e larboro del buxolo, zoe folto, & la soa foglia e quasi como q'lla della ca'nella, ma e un poco piu to'da, & e de quel colore co'e gia uedissi in Zeilani, la quale e quasi como la foglia d'l lauro. Q'n' so'no maturi quisti garoffoli, li dicti ho'i li sbatteno co' le ca'ne, & metteno sotto al dicto arbore alcune store per racoglierli La terra doue so'no quisti arbori e come arena, zoe de quel medesmo colore, no' pero che sia arena. El paese si e molto basso, & de qui no' se uede la stella tramo'tana. Veduto ch' hauessemo questa insula & questa ge'te dima'da'mo alli xp'iani se altro ce era da ueder' Ce resposero, uediamo un pocho in ch' modo ue'deno questi garoffoli: troua'mo che se ue'deuano al dopio piu che le noce moscate pure a mesura, p'che quelle p'sone no' inte'deno pesi."—Ludouico de Varthema.[1]

(2)

"Auiendo el papa Alexandro sexto repartido las conquistas del nueuo mundo, à los reyes de Castilla y Portugal, hizieron de acuerdo la particion, por vna linea q' cosmografos echaron al mundo; paraq', el vno a la parte del ocidente, y el otro, a la del oriente, siguiesen sus descubrimientos y conquistas, pacifica'do lo que cada vno ganase dentro de su demarcacion.

[[1] *Itinerario de Ludouico de Varthema Bolognese nello Egypto, nella Surria, nella Arabia deserta & felice, nella Persia, nella India, & nella Ethiopia*, etc. Roma, M.D.X. 4°. f. 79.]

Despues, que por la corona de Portugal se ganó la ciudad de Malaca, en la tierra firme de la Asia, en el reyno de Ior, llamada por los antiguos Aureachersoneso, el an'o de mil y quinientos y onze, a las nueuas de las islas q' caen cerca, especialme'te, las del Maluco y Banda, donde se coge el clauo y la nuez moscada; salio vna armada de Portugueses a su descubrimiento, q' auiendo estado en Banda, fuero' de alli lleuados à la isla de Terrenate, vna de las del Maluco, por el mismo rey della, en defensa suya, contra el de Tidore su vezino, çon quien tenia guerra, q' fue principio del asiento que los Portugueses hizieron en el Maluco.

Fra'cisco Serrano (q' boluio a Malaca con este descubrimie'to, y passó à la India, para yr a Portugal à dar quenta del) murio antes de hazer este viaje, auiendo comunicado por cartas a su amigo Fernando de Magallanes (q' se auian hallado juntos en la toma de Malaca y estaua en Portugal) lo que auia visto; con cuyas relaciones, entendio lo q' conuenia del descubrimiento y nauegacion à estas islas."—ANTONIO DE MORGA.[1]

---

(3)

" Las islas que tiene la especería del clavo son estas, Terrenate, Tidori, Motil, Maquian, Bachan: estas son las principales.

Terrenate es alta y toda poblada al rededor, y el pueblo principal que se dice Terrenate, está por la parte del sudueste: esta isla es alta, que está mas al norte de todas, y los árboles de clavo están arriba en mitad de la montan'a, cógese cada an'o mill bahares de clavo que son 4^{M} quintales; esto se entiende como en Castilla, cuando hay buena vendeja del vino: esta isla de Terrenate tiene otra isla pequen'a al nornordeste, llámase Iri, es poblada: tiene esta isla de Terrenate 9 leguas.

La isla de Tidori es alta mas que la de Terrenate, y mas aguda para arriba, tiene una falda al nornordeste, es poblada toda al derredor, y el pueblo principal que se llama Tidori está por la parte del leste: córrese con la isla de Lornate norte sur cuarta de nordeste sudueste, una legua escasa; los árboles del clavo son arriba en medio de la montan'a: cógese en esta isla de Tidori novecientos ballares

[[1] *Svcesos de las Islas Philipinas. Dirigidos a don Christoval Gomez de Sandoval y Rojas dvqve de Cea por el doctor Antonio de Morga.* Mexici ad Indos. Anno 1609. 4°.]

de clavo, que son tres mil é seiscientos quintales, y es mejor que lo de Terrenate: tiene de rodeo nueve leguas. Esta isla tiene otra pequen'a al suduеste que se dice Meytara, hay un cuarto de legua desta isla allá. Tiene otra isla esta isla de Tidori al susudueste que se dice Mare; hay una legua de la una á la otra: tiene 4 leguas de rodeo: hay algun poco de clavo, y es bravo y agora le empieza á hacer bueno, y está esta dicha isla de Tidori en dos tercios de grado de la banda del norte.

La isla de Motil no es tan grande como esta de Tidori, ni tan alta, ansimismo se cria el clavo en lo alto como en esta otras: cógese en ella ochocientos ballares de clavo, que sons tres mil y doscientos quintales: córrese con esta isla de Tidori norte sur, hay tres leguas.

La isla de Maquian es algo mayor que la de Motil y cógese en ella ochocientos ballares de clavo, que es muy bueno: córrese con esta isla de Motil norte sur: hay una legua desta isla de Maquian: al sueste de Maquian hay una isla que se corre al sueste: llámase Cayoan.

La isla de Bachan está mas al sur de todas estas islas ya dichas, mas de 8 leguas, y es mayor que ninguna de las dichas: cógese en ella quinientos ballares de clavo, que son dos mil quintales: no es tan bueno como el de estotras islas, y causalo que está apartada de la línea mas que las otras."—HERNANDO DE LA TORRE.[1]

[[1] *Coleccion de los viages y děscubrimientos que hicieron por mar los Españoles desde fines del siglo* XV. *Coordinada é ilustrada por D. Martin Fernandez de Navarrete*, etc. Madrid, 1825-37. 4o. v. 286.]

(1.)

A chapter of the Island of *Monoch*, where cloves grow.

We landed on this island of *Monoch*, which is much smaller than *Bandan*, but the inhabitants are worse than those of *Bandan*, yet live in the same manner, and are rather fairer, and the air is rather cooler. Here cloves grow, and in many other small uninhabited islands which lie near it. The tree which bears cloves is thick and bushy like the box-tree, and its leaf resembles that of the cinnamon-tree, but is more round, and of the colour of those which we had already seen in *Zeilani*, which is like the leaf of the laurel. When the cloves are ripe, the said men beat them down with canes, placing mats under the trees to catch them. The soil in which the trees grow is like sand; that is, of the same colour, but it is not sand. The country is very low [as to latitude], and they never see the north star. Having thus seen the island and its inhabitants, we asked if any other christians had been seen there. They answered, we saw a few, by which means we sold our cloves. We found that cloves sold twice as dear as nutmegs, but by measure, as these persons do not understand weights.—Ludouico de Varthema, 1510.

(2.)

Pope Alexander the Sixth, having divided the conquests of the new world between the kings of *Castilla* and *Portugal*, made the division, with their consent, by a meridian which geographers announced to the world, to the effect that each, one to the westward and the other to the eastward, should pursue his own discoveries and conquests, and retain in peace what he had acquired within the line of demarcation.

After the Portuguese had won the city of *Malaca*, on the continent of *Asia*, in the kingdom of *Jor*—called by the ancients *Aureachersoneso*—in consequence of the receipt of intelligence of the islands in those seas, and especially of those of *Maluco* and *Banda*, whence cloves and nutmegs are procured, a fleet of ships was despatched in 1511 in order to discover them, and having staid some time in *Banda*, they were thence conducted to the island of *Terrenate*, one of the *Maluco* islands, by the king himself, in his own defence against his neighbour the king of *Tidore*, with whom he was at war, and this was the first settlement which the Portuguese made in the *Maluco* islands.

Francisco Serrano, who returned to *Malaca* with this expedition, and proceeded to *India* on his way to *Portugal* to give an account of it, died before he made the voyage, having communicated by letters to his friend *Fernando de Magallanes*, who had been his associate in the taking of *Malaca*, and was then in *Portugal*, all that he had seen; from whose statements he learned what suited his purpose with regard to the discovery and navigation of these islands.—ANTONIO DE MORGA, 1609.

(3.)

The islands which produce the spice called cloves are *Terrenate*, *Tidori*, *Motil*, *Maquian*, and *Bachan*. These are the principal islands.

Terrenate is high land, and inhabited all round the coast, and the principal town, which is called *Terrenate*, is on the south-west side. This lofty island is to the northward of the others, and the clove-trees are half-way up the hill. They gather a thousand bahars of cloves in the year, which make four thousand quintals: this is to be understood as in *Castilla*, when there is a good vintage. The island of *Terrenate* has another small island bearing north-north-east of it, which is called *Iri*, and is inhabited. The island of *Terrenate* is nine leagues in circumference.

The island of *Tidori* is higher than *Terrenate*, and more piked towards its summit, with a slope to the north-north-east. It is inhabited all round, and the principal town, which is called *Tidori*, is on the east side. It bears with the island of *Lornate* [Terrenate?] north and south and a point to the north-east and south-west, at the distance of a short league. The clove-trees are half-way up the hill. They gather in this island of *Tidori* nine hundred bahars of cloves, which make three thousand six hundred quintals, and it is of better quality than that of *Terrenate*. It is nine leagues round. This island has another small island to the south-west, which is called *Meytara*, at the distance of a quarter of a league.

This island of *Tidori* has another small island to the south-south-west, which is called *Mare*, at the distance of a league. It is four leagues round. It has some few clove-trees, which grow wild, but they now begin to improve them; and this said island is in two-thirds of a degree of north latitude.

The island of *Motil* is not so large as *Tidori*, nor so high, but the clove-trees grow on the high ground in the same manner as in the other islands. They gather here eight hundred bahars of cloves, which make three thousand two hundred quintals. This island and *Tidori* bear north and south from each other, at the distance of three leagues.

The island of *Maquian* is somewhat larger than *Motil*, and they gather here eight hundred bahars of cloves, which are very good. This island and *Motil* bear north and south, at the distance of a league. To the south-east of *Maquian* there is an island which runs in a south-eastern direction. It is called *Cayoan*.

The island of *Bachan* is more to the southward than all the aforesaid islands, more by eight leagues, and is larger than any of them. They gather here five hundred bahars of cloves, which make two thousand quintals. The cloves are not so good as in the other islands, because it is further from the equinoctial line.—HERNANDO DE LA TORRE, 1527.

"OF THE ILAND OF MALUCO.

The Ilandes of Maluco are fiue, viz. Maluco, Tarnate, Tydor, Geloulo, and an other where the Portingales haue 2 forts, that is in Tarnate and Tydor, which long since were discouered and wonne, where they trafficke from Malacca and out of India. The Spaniards haue sought diuers meanes to haue traffique there, and came from thence out of Noua Spaigne, into the iland called Tarnate, where in a storme they lost their shippe, and so could not get from thence againe, whereby they were by the Portingales most of them slayne, and the rest taken and sent prisoners into Portingale, whereupon the king of Spaine and Portingale had a long quarrell and contention, touching the diuision of their conquests, and discouery of the seas, which by the Popes meanes at the last was ended, in such sort, that at this present onely the Portingale trafickes to those ilands. These ilands haue no other spice then cloues, but in so great abundance, that as it appeareth, by them the whole world is filled therewith. In this iland are found firie hilles, they are very dry and burnt land, they haue nothing els but victuals of flesh and fish, but for rice, corne, onyons, garlicke, and such like, and all other necessaries, some are brought from Portingale, and some from other places thereabout, which they take and barter for cloues. The bread which they haue there of their owne baking is of wood or rootes, like the men of Brasillia, and their cloathes are of wouen strawe or herbes, faire to the eye: in these ilands onlie is found the bird, which the Portingales call *passaros de sol,* that is fowle of the sunne, the Italians call it *manu codiatas,* and the Latinists, *paradiseas,* and by vs called paradice birdes, for y[e] beauty of their feathers which passe al other birds: these birds are neuer seene aliue, but being dead they are found vpon the iland: they flie, as it is said, alwaies into the sunne, and keepe themselues continually in the ayre, without lighting on the earth, for they haue neither feet nor wings, but onely head and body, and the most part tayle, as appeareth by the birdes that are brought from thence into India, and some from thence hether, but not many, for they are costlie. I brought two of them with me, for doctor Paludanus, which were male and female, which I gaue vnto him, for his chamber. These ilands lie among diuers other ilands, and because there is no speciall notice of them, by reason of the small conuersation with them: I let them passe, and turne again vnto the coast of Malacca, which I left at the Cape of Singapura, and so will shewe the coast along."—IOHN HVIGHEN VAN LINSCHOTEN, 1598.

LIST OF AUTHORITIES CITED IN THE NOTES.

" L'exactitude scrupuleuse est le premier mérite, comme le premier devoir, d'un bibliographe."—Charles MAGNIN.

*** *The names and short titles which precede the descriptions of the authorities are given precisely as they stand in the notes, and the numbers which follow refer to those notes. By this method, which may seem rather novel, much useless repetition has been avoided. As some of the works are framed chronologically, others alphabetically, and others furnished with indexes, I dispense with minute references.*

The titles of the books are copied literatim *as far as the elliptic marks, and are to be considered as entire when no such marks are inserted. The names of the authors, and the titular distinctions which precede those names, are also copied* literatim. *The designations which follow the names, or portions of those designations, are given when they serve to identify the authors, or to intimate their qualifications with reference to the works in question. The number of the edition, if stated, is repeated. The imprints of the books are abbreviated. The size, and the number of volumes, follow the imprints.*

The elliptic marks used are the — and an *etc. Additions and corrections, if derived from the books themselves, are given as parentheses; if derived from other sources, in brackets. Doubtful particulars have a note of interrogation affixed.*

India-House Mss.——India-House manuscripts. Note 1, 2, 162. See also *Instructions*, *Appendix*, and the table of contents.

Stow.——The annales of England. Faithfully collected out of the most autenticall authors, *etc.*—by Iohn Stow citizen of London. *London*, (1605). 4to. Note 2, 148.

Registrum Roffense.——Registrum Roffense: or, a collection of antient records, charters, and instruments—of the diocese of Rochester. By John Thorpe, M.D. *London*, 1769. Folio. Note 2.

Charters E. I. C.——Charters granted to the East-India Company, from 1601 (1600); *etc.* [*London*, 1772?] 4to. Note 3.

Sir H. Manwayring.——The sea-mans dictionary—by sir Henry Manwayring, knight. *London*, 1644. 4to. Note 4, 48.

W. Falconer.——An universal dictionary of the marine—by William Falconer, author of *The shipwreck. London*, 1769. 4to. Note 8, 10, 69, 72.

T. Clayborne.——The second voyage set forth by the Company into the East-Indies—written by Thomas Clayborne. Purchas vol. i. Note 9, 12, 15, 17, 19, 21, 24, 40, 43, 55, 64, 95, 99, 154, 157, 159, 161.

Capt. Davis.——The worldes hydrographical discription—published by I. Dauis, of Sandrudg by Dartmouth. *London*, 1595. 16mo. Note 11.

Instructions.——(*Appendix* No. III.) Note 11, 23, 26, 45, 57, 60, 83, 91, 92.

Hakluyt.——The principal navigations, voiages, traffiqves and discoueries of the English nation—by Richard Haklvyt, M.A. *London*, 1598-1600. Folio. 3 vols. Note 14, 22, 29.

Purchas.——Haklvytvs posthumus, or Pvrchas his pilgrimes. Contayning a history of the world, in sea voyages and lande-trauells by Englishmen and others.—By Samvel Pvrchas, B.D. *London*, 1625. Folio. 4 vols. Note 18, 20, 22, 33, 35, 37, 41, 61, 73, 122, 131, 149.

De Barros——Da Asia de João de Barros—dos feitos, que os Portuguezes fizeram no descubrimento, e conquista dos mares, e terras do Oriente. —Nova edição. *Lisboa*, 1777-8. 8vo. 9 vols. Note 22, 152.

Lieut. Vidal.——Survey of the Cape of Good Hope. By Lieut. A. T. E. Vidal, and others, 1822. Admiralty chart, 1828. Note 27.

Nares.——A glossary; or, collection of words, phrases, names, *etc.*, which have been thought to require illustration. By Robert Nares, A.M. *London*, 1822. 4to. Note 28, 118.

J. O. Halliwell.——A dictionary of archaic and provincial words, *etc.* By James Orchard Halliwell, F.R.S. *London*, 1847. 8vo. 2 vols. Note 31.

Sir R. Hawkins.——The observations of sir Richard Hawkins knight, in his voiage into the South Sea. Anno Domini 1593. *London*, 1622. Folio. Note 34, 44, 125, 158.

Viscount Wimbledon.——A iovrnall, and relation of the action—on the coast of Spaine, 1625. (By Edward viscount Wimbledon.) Printed in the yeere 1627. 4to. Note 38, 47.

English expositor.——An English expositor: teaching the interpretation of the hardest words used in our language.—By I. B. (John Bullokar.) *London*, 1641. 12mo. Note 42, 134, 162.

Roteiro.——Roteiro da viagem que em descobrimento da India pelo Cabo da Boa Esperança fez dom Vasco da Gama em 1497. *Porto*, 1838. 8vo. Note 44.

Jean Mocquet.——Voyages en Afriqve, Asie, Indes Orientales et Occidentales. Faits par Iean Mocqvet, garde du cabinet des singularitez du roy. *A Paris*, 1617. 8vo. Note 44.

J. Horsburgh.——India directory, or directions for sailing to and from the East Indies, China, *etc.* By James Horsburgh, F.R.S., hydrographer to the honorable East India Company. Third edition. *London*, 1826-7. 4to. 2 vols. Note 46, 68, 93, 111.

Edmund Scott.——An exact discovrse of the subtilties, fashions, pollicies, religion, and ceremonies of the East Indians—Written by Edmund Scott. *London*, 1606. 4to. Note 49, 54, 56, 58, 60, 62, 63, 77, 78, 82, 84, 105, 110, 147, 149, 153, 156.

C. de Renneville.——Recueil des voiages qui ont servi à l'établissement et aux progrès de la Compagnie des Indes Orientales, formée dans les provinces-unies des Païs-Bas. (par De Constantin.) Seconde édition. *A Amsterdam*, 1725. 12mo. 7 vols. Note 50, 51, 52, 61, 70, 71, 84, 88, 103, 107, 115, 121, 123, 124, 133, 136, 140, 150.

W. Marsden.——A dictionary of the Malayan language—by William Marsden, F.R.S. *London*, 1812. 4to. Note 53, 62, 87, 101, 102, 108, 143.

Capt. Smith.——A sea grammar, with the plaine exposition of Smiths *Accidence for young sea-men*, enlarged.—Written by captaine Iohn Smith. *London*, 1627. 4to. Note 59, 74, 112, 113, 126, 135, 160.

Sir W. Ralegh.——The discoverie of the large, rich and bewtifvl empire of Gviana——performed in the yeare 1595. by sir W. Ralegh knight. *London*, 1596. 4to. Note 66, 76, 79.

Linschoten.——Iohn Hvighen van Linschoten his discours of voyages into ye Easte and West Indies—from the Dutch by W. P. [Phillip]. *London*, (1598). Folio. Note 68.

L. de Argensola.——Conqvista de las Islas Malvcas—escrita por el licenciado Bartolome Leonardo de Argensola. En *Madrid*, 1609. Folio. Note 77, 104, 132, 143.

[Alex. Dalrymple.]—Plan of the Island Amboina. From a Ms. 1782. Admiralty Chart. Note 80.

Manoel de Faria y Sousa.——The Portugues Asia: or, the history of the discovery and conquest of India—from the Spanish of Manuel de Faria y Sousa by John Stevens. *London*, 1695. 8vo. 3 vols. Note 81, 88, 90, 123, 142.

Articles of peace.——Articles of peace, entercovrse, and commerce—concluded between James I. and Philip III. of Spain. *London*, 1605. 4to. Note 82.

Rogers Ruding.——Annals of the coinage of Great Britain and its dependencies—by the rev. Rogers Ruding, F.S.A. Third edition. *London*, 1840. 4to. 3 vols. Note 89.

D'Aprés de Mannevillette. —— Instructions sur la navigation des Indes Orientales et de la Chine—par M. d'Aprés de Mannevillette. *A Brest*, 1775. 4to. Note 93.

The world encompassed.——The world encompassed by sir Francis Drake—collected out of the notes of master Francis Fletcher, and others. *London*, 1628. 4to. Note 97, 104, 128, 152.

[Derfelden van Hinderstein.] Algemeene Kaart van Nederlandsch Oostindie —door G. F. Baron von Derfelden van Hinderstein. 1842. Nine sheets.

Island princess.——Comedies and tragedies written by Francis Beavmont and Iohn Fletcher—*London*, 1647. Folio. Note 100.

A. Jal.——Archéologie navale, par A. Jal, historiographe de la marine. *Paris*, 1840. 8vo. 2 vols. Note 106.

S. de Villamont.——Les voyages dv seignevr de Villamont, cheualier de l'ordre de Hierusalem.—en Italie, Grece, Syrie, *etc.* *A Paris*, 1598. 8vo. Note 106.

Appendix.——(See table of contents.) Note 109, 119, 153.

Dialogves.——Dialogves in the English and Malaiane langvages—translated from Gotardvs Arthvsivs by Avgvstine Spalding, merchant. *London*, 1614. Small 4to. Note 110.

W. Welwod.——An abridgement of all sea-lawes—by William Welwod, professor of the ciuill lawe. *London*, 1613. 4to. Note 127.

Pigafetta.——Premier voyage autour du monde, par le chev[r]. Pigafetta, sur l'escadre de Magellan, pendant les années 1519-22. *Paris*, l'an ix. 8vo. Note 128.

R. Carew.——The svrvey of Cornwall. Written by Richard Carew of Antonie, esquire. *London*, 1602. 4to. Note 129.

Robert Coverte.——A trve and almost incredible report of an Englishman—cast away in Cambaya, *etc.* By captaine Robert Couerte. *London*, 1612. 4to. Note 131.

Lewes Roberts.——The merchants mappe of commerce : wherein, the vniversall manner and matter of trade, is compendiously handled.—by Lewes Roberts, merchant. *London*, 1638. Folio. Note 141.

Capt. Barwick.——A breefe discourse, concerning the force and effect of all manuall weapons of fire, *etc.* Written by Humfrey Barwick, captaine, *et encor plus oultre*. *London*, 4to. n. d. Note 145.

R. Barret.——The theorike and practike of moderne warres—written by Robert Barret. *London*, 1598. Folio. Note 146.

Andrew Borde.——The fyrst boke of the introduction of knowledge—made by Andrew Borde, of phisicke doctor. *London*, 4to. Reprint. Note 147.

Henry Peacham.——The compleat gentleman, fashioning him absolute—by Henry Peacham, M.A. *London*, 1622. 4to. Note 151.

D. Belchier.—Hans Beer-Pot his invisible comedie, of see me, and see me not—(By Dabridgecourt Belchier.) *London*, 1618. 4to. Note 151.

INDEX OF PERSONS, PLACES, PRINCIPAL SUBJECTS, AND UNCOMMON WORDS OR PHRASES.

*** This index is limited to the narrative which forms the text of the volume. The journal of Thomas Clayborne is given in notes 9, 12, 15, 17, 19, 21, 24, 40, 43, 55, 64, 95, 99, 154, 157, 159, and 161. An interrogation implies uncertainty; the mark = indicates synonyms; *Ob.* stands for *Obiit.* The glossarial items, printed in *italics*, refer to the pages in which the words and phrases are explained.

CORRIGENDA.

P. 20, note 69, read *been*; p. 26, note 88, read *canonnèrent*; p. 40, line 19, read *a-clock*; p. 73, line 20, read *Gegogoe*.

FINIS.

T. RICHARDS, 37 GREAT QUEEN STREET.

For EU product safety concerns, contact us at Calle de José Abascal, 56–1°, 28003 Madrid, Spain or eugpsr@cambridge.org.

www.ingramcontent.com/pod-product-compliance
Ingram Content Group UK Ltd.
Pitfield, Milton Keynes, MK11 3LW, UK
UKHW012342130625
459647UK00009B/478